Guide

D0253486

Institut de
cultura ∎

Guide

CLAUSTRE RAFART I PLANAS,
Curator of the Museu Picasso de Barcelona

Ajuntament de Barcelona

Museu Picasso de Barcelona
Montcada, 15-19
08003 Barcelona
Phone 93 319 63 10
Fax 93 315 01 02
Opening times: Tuesday to Saturday and holidays, 10 to 20 h. Sundays, 10
to 15 h. Closed Mondays.

Photographs:
AHCB-ARXIU FOTOGRÀFIC
4.263; 4.265; 4.266; 4.268; 10.941; 70.232; 70.464; 70.477; 110.009;
110.011; 110.018; 110.053; 110.058; 110.066; 110.281; 112.028;
112.750
AHCB-ARXIU FOTOGRÀFIC. Jordi Calafell
70.489; 110.028
AHCB-ARXIU FOTOGRÀFIC. Jordi Calafell - Rosa Feliu
4.270; 4.272; 4.275; 45.006; 70.241; 70.456; 70.459; 70.460; 70.465;
70.471; 70.472; 110.001; 110.016; 110.046;
AHCB-ARXIU FOTOGRÀFIC. Rosa Feliu
110.872
AHCB-ARXIU FOTOGRÀFIC. Ramon Muro
4.274; 70.226; 70.243; 70.433; 70.450; 110.006; 110.008; 110.010;
110.013; 110020; 110.073; 110.213; 112.761;
MUSEU PICASSO. BARCELONA. Ramon Manent
4.267; 4271; 4.273; 70.810; 110.004; 110.011; 110.012; 110.029;
112.867;
MUSEU PICASSO. BARCELONA
70.244; 112.446; 112.450; 112.770;
MUSEU PICASSO. BARCELONA. Gasull Fotografia
4.269; 70.435; 70.449;
© Photo R.M.N.

© publication Ajuntament de Barcelona
© text Claustre Rafart i Planas, curator MPB
© works Heirs of Pablo Picasso, VEGAP. Barcelona
Published by: Ajuntament de Barcelona
Direcció de Serveis Editorials
Editorial coordination: Jordi Fernando
Graphic design and layout: Marina Vilageliu / Montserrat Coma
English: Valerie Collins
Films and printing: Impremta Municipal
Dossier number: 006/98
ISBN 84-7609 - 876 - 6
Legal Deposit: B. 12.705.1998

Contents

Presentation

■

The Museu Picasso de Barcelona is a living testimony to the links that bound Picasso to the city of Barcelona. When Picasso was not much more than a teenage boy learning the artist's craft, he arrived in a Barcelona that was bubbling over with Modernist fervour, a city setting its sights on a Europe brimming with exciting ventures. A Barcelona at the epicentre of the great shockwave set off by the Industrial Revolution, the city enlargement project and the demolition of the walls. A Barcelona eager to take its place as one of Europe's leading cities.

Two factors determined Picasso's close relationship with Barcelona and at the same time underpinned the Museum itself: the years he actually spent in the city (1895-1904) and his relationships here: family and friends.

The story of the Museu Picasso is the story of the artist's steadfast wish to leave the mark of his art on the city that opened the doors of modernity to him. This art is now here for us to enjoy, work after work, in the unrivalled setting of the palaces on Carrer Montcada, a splendid setting in itself. So the Museum stands as the union of the art of several centuries, forming an exceptional heritage which puts Barcelona in a unique position on the international art scene.

This guidebook fulfils one of the basic purposes of any museum, which is to acquaint visitors with its permanent collections, and as such is an invitation to discover the rich heritage of the Museu Picasso of Barcelona.

Joan Clos i Matheu
Mayor of Barcelona

Jaume Sabartés in Barcelona i Roda el món i torna al Born.
Cannes, 6 September 1956. Red and blue pencil on paper.

Introduction. "Roda el món i torna al Born"*

Picasso's relationship with Barcelona dates to the end of the 19th century, when his initial encounter with the city led to an attachment that was to prove decisive for the art of the 20th century.

For the young Pablo, the arrival in Barcelona of the Ruiz Picasso family in September 1895 was a chance to make contact with a new cultural milieu which would spark his latent creativity. In the arts. Turn-of-the-century Barcelona was in a restless ferment, open to anything that involved innovation, and desperately eager to join in the movements that held sway over the aesthetic canons of Europe: for Pablo Ruiz Picasso this meant an encounter with modernity. It was the ideal setting for the young man to start to define his personality as an artist and also to strike up friendships to share his artistic and personal concerns.

One of the relationships begun during this youthful period in Barcelona would eventually be the origin of the Picasso Museum. Jaume Sabartés was one of those friends made when lifelong friendships were forged; he became Picasso's personal secretary in 1935 and one of the people closest to him. So it is no surprise that in the late 50s the two should agree to meet again in the city where they first met, and together, to embody the Catalan proverb *Roda el món i torna al Born*. And they were agreed upon returning to the Born neighbourhood to create a Picasso Museum which in the thirty-five years since its inception has become one of the city's key places.

The collections, which are discussed by Claustre Rafart in this book, are a reflection of what Barcelona gave Picasso and an unrivalled exponent of the art of his formative years, as well as that of later periods, giving us an in

9

sight into the mature work of one of the 20th century's greatest artists.

Maria Teresa Ocaña
Director

*Catalan proverb, with deep roots in Barcelona's traditions, meaning that after travelling the world, true happiness is to be found in returning to one's origins: "There's no place like home".

History of the buildings

In the mid-12th century, Barcelona was still enclosed within the walls of the Roman city. Lacking vital space to expand, new nuclei of dwellings and factories began to spring up outside the wall, known as *bòries* or *viles noves* (new towns). At the north-west exit from the city, on the site of what is now the Plaça del Àngel, the most important of these developed: *Mercadal*. Not so far away, by the sea —the natural element for certain factories— Vilanova de la Mar took shape. These two centres, which were the largest and liveliest, were linked by a street, the carrer de Montcada, which was just beginning to be developed.

Carrer de Montcada followed the route of the old path that linked the port with the road to Rome, which left the city by the north-east gate. The junction was on the site of the small Romanesque church of Marcús (12th century).

In the second half of the 13th century, the real work of developing the area was undertaken. On Carrer de Montcada important buildings, palaces and mansions of courtiers, mer-

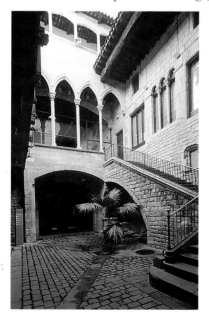

chants and burghers progressively went up. As a general rule, those built in the course of the 13th and 14th centuries had a rectangular courtyard surrounded with corridors with an outside staircase leading to the main first floor, the owner's residence. On the ground floor were the kitchens, storerooms, stables, and so on. The top floor housed the attics and servants' quarters.

Floors, turrets and facades were built with ashlars, while for the rest of the building good quality adobe wall with a thickness of 57 centimetres was used. From the 15th century on, unworked stone and brick with lime mortar became more widely used and gradually replaced adobe. This was complemented with excellent artisan joinery in the mouldings —3th and 14th centuries— which shows that the workers of period were acquainted with the Moorish tradition.

The Picasso Museum is housed in three of these palaces: the Aguilar, the Baró de Castellet, and the Meca. All three are constructions of medieval origin which later underwent major transformations.

From the documentary point of view, Joan Ainaud lamented that the loss of the private archives and notarial documents from before 1300 made the study of the initial history of the palaces on this street difficult.

The Aguilar Palace still bears the name of the merchant Berenguer d'Aguilar who bought the building from Constança, the wife of Ramon Desplà, on 23 November 1400. There are still remains from the 13th century of the old residence of Jaume Ses Fonts. The painted ceilings and mural decoration are from that century. In 1961, when the plastering of a room was removed, there appeared remains of 13th century mural paintings, in particular one depicting the conquest of Mallorca by James I in 1229. One of the most important historical representations extant in Catalonia, it is now in the National Art Museum of Catalonia. The heraldic motifs on the

ceilings, mainly caldrons and roses, led Joan Ainaud to suppose that the building must have originally belonged to the Calders lines and later to the Desvalls. Later, it passed to Ponç de Lledó, a personage at the court of the king of Aragon and in 1335 was bought by the powerful merchant Pere de Mitjavila, who made major changes to it, as did his successors. Later, in 1386, the palace belonged to the Coromines-Desplà family, members of the high Barcelona bourgeoisie, who sold it to the Aguilars. Successive generations of Aguilars remodelled it, leaving on the building the marks of the most varied styles.

The last direct heir to the name Aguilar was Dionísia, the wife of Cristòfol

d'Ocart de Queralt, an ancestor of the second branch of the counts of Santa Coloma. The palace was known with this title until it was sold, in 1837, to two eminent members of the new Catalan bourgeoisie: Pere Clerch i Rossinyol and his son-in-law Llorenç Pons i Fo. Finally, on 3 November 1953, Barcelona City Council purchased it from the Pons family.

The palace of the Baron of Castellet takes its names from the title that Charles IV granted in 1797 to Marià Alegre d'Aparici i d'Amat, proprietor and renovator of the building purchased on 16 June 1722 by his forbear Miquel Alegre. The history of the owners of the building, however, dates back to the 13th and 14th centuries. In the 14th century it belonged successively to the Ravós and Branca families. In the 15th century it was the property of the Gerona family. In 1531, Angelina Gerona sold it to Domènec Moradell. Later, through purchases and inheritances, the palace passed to the Corrego, Lluch, Ripoll and Llinàs families.

The Alegres carried out several renovations, the most important being the neoclassical room built by the Baron of Castellet in the mid-18th century. The blend of classical and baroque elements give the room the sumptuousness typical of the international classicism which, according to Joan Ainaud, the baron had become acquainted with at the court of St Petersburg in 1790. Upon his death in 1831 he bequeathed it to the Hospital of the Holy Cross. When his widow died in 1834, the building was rented by various tenants and finally bought by the Rius family. In the fifties, it became the property of Barcelona City Council.

The history of the Meca Palace is similar to that of the other two buildings that form the Picasso Museum. Our earliest documentation dates to the year 1349. It shows that the palace was sold by the administrators of the Hospìtal of Pere Desvilar, located in the Ribera neighbourhood, to Jaume Cavaller, chief councillor of Barcelona City Council. His daughter Felipona married the politician Ramon Desplà, and their son

Ramon Desplà i Cavaller, who also became chief councillor, turned the Desplà Palace into the most important building in the entire block. Then it passed successively to the Cervelló, Mur, Torrella and Santjust families, and finally, in the 16th century, to the Cassadors or Caçadors and their successors, the marquises of Ciutadilla, the first of whom was Josep Meca i Caçador. The members of this line kept it until the widow of Josep Meca sold it to the merchant Segimon Milans in 1719. The Milans family were behind the major renovation of the building carried out in the 17th century. Subsequently it passed into the hands of the Vidals and then the Monegals. The latter bequeathed it to the Brothers of the Christian Doctrine. In 1901 it became home to the Montepío de Santa Madrona, which was incorporated into the social welfare department of a bank. On 5 December 1977 the bank and Barcelona City Council signed a leasing agreement for the palace running until the year 2007. Thanks to this agreement, in 1981 the project to renovate and extend the Picasso Museum was begun, and the Museum was finally opened on 11 January 1982. The renovation work joined the Meca Palace with the Aguilar and the Baró del Castellet to form a major complex, which has recently been enlarged with the addition of two neighbouring buildings, the former Casa Maurí and the Finestres Palace.

The Picasso Museum is located in an unparalelled setting, in the most emblematic street of the La Ribera neigbourhood, carrer Montcada, at the end of which stands one of the most beautiful Gothic churches in Catalonia: Santa Maria del Mar.

Close to the Museum is Picasso's Barcelona, the places where he lived with his family between 1895 and 1904, the La Llotja School of Fine Arts where he completed his formal training, the studios where he painted, and last but not least, the places where he and his friends used to go for amusement and entertainment.

History of a collection

The Picasso Museum of Barcelona opened its doors to the public on 9 March 1963. The initial stocks were formed by the collection of Picasso's works from the Art Museums of Barcelona and the donations of Jaume Sabartés, Picasso's friend and secretary.

The former was begun in 1919, when Picasso gave *The Harlequin* (1917) to the city of Barcelona. This oil was one of the eight works by Picasso in the art exhibition organised by Barcelona City Council and the origin of a collection which was to form one of the most important in the world.

In 1932, Barcelona City Council and the Generalitat de Catalunya (Autonomous Government) acquired the Plandiura Collection, one of the most valuable private art collections in Catalunya, which included 22 works by Picasso. Two years later the Art Museum of Catalunya opened a room devoted to Picasso with the Plandiura Collection and *The Harlequin*, in the National Palace of Montjuïc. This was visited by Picasso shortly before the inauguration.

In successive years until the Museum opened, the collection grew, with prints and drawings donated by Picasso himself and by Catalan collectors and with works purchased by the Council.

In 1957, thanks to Picasso's interest and the contributions of Jaume Sabartés, the possibility of creating a Picasso Museum was raised. From then on the relationship between Picasso and Barcelona was strengthened.

The opening of the Museum encouraged the collectors to help to increase its stocks and the Council itself, stimulated by the Museum, bought works sporadically.

1968 saw the death in Paris of Jaume Sabartés, to whom Picasso paid tribute with a major donation to the Museum. First he committed himself to

giving a copy of every print he produced from then until his death. Many of these prints bear a dedication to Sabartés. Then he donated the blue portrait of his friend —painted in the autum of 1901 in Paris— and the entire *Las Meninas* series (1957), his interpretation of the Velázquez masterpiece. The suite is formed of 58 oils, 44 free interpretations of the baroque original, 9 oils devoted to *The Pigeons*, 3 landscapes and 2 free interpretations. It is the only interpretative series produced by Picasso to have been assembled in its entirety in a museum.

In 1970 Picasso gave the city of Barcelona a magnificent donation which made the Museum the world's most important centre for the artist's formative years: the work kept for three generations by his family, mother María Picasso López, sister Dolores Ruiz Picasso, and nieces and nephews, the Vilató family. The donation comprises 82 oils on canvas, 110 oils on panel and 21 on other supports, 681 drawings, pastels and water colours on paper, 17 albums, 4 books with drawings in the margins, 1 etching and 5 miscellaneous objects. The works were delivered to the Council on 8 May and exhibited on 18 December of that year.

The following year the Picasso Museum launched a policy of temporary exhibitions, organised and produced by the Museum itself or with the cooperation of other institutions. The exhibitions, which enjoyed a greater impetus from 1983, followed two well defined lines, one aimed at popularising Picasso's life and work, and the other focussing on providing knowledge of the artists and artistic styles which in one way or another have had contact with Picasso. Alongside the exhibitions, seminars on Picassian studies and talks on subjects of major cultural importance consolidate the Museum's prestige.

THE MUSEU PICASSO OF BARCELONA

COLLECTIONS

The formative years: 1891-1899

■

| 1881 | 25 October | Málaga, birth of Pablo Ruiz Picasso, first child of José Ruiz Blasco, painter and teacher at San Telmo School of Fine Arts and curator of the Municipal Museum, and María Picasso López. |

1884	28 December	Birth of Dolores (Lola) Ruiz Picasso.
1887	30 October	Birth of Concepción (Conchita) Ruiz Picasso
1891	September	Family moves to La Corunya where José Ruiz appointed lecturer at School of Fine Arts. Pablo enrols at La Guarda High School.
1892		Pablo starts studying art at the School of Fine Arts.
1895	January	Conchita dies of diphtheria
	April	José Ruiz moves to Barcelona to take up lecturing post at La Llotja School of Fine Arts.
	Summer	Holidays in Málaga. Stopover in Madrid.
	End September	Family moves to Barcelona, to carrer Cristina, 3. La Llotja entrance examination, where studies for two years.

19

1896	*Summer*	Family holiday in Málaga. Return to Barcelona. Move to carrer de la Mercè, 32. José rents Pablo's first studio at carrer de la Plata, 4.
	October	Academic year begins
1897	*Summer*	Family holiday in Málaga
	October	Begins studies at San Fernando Academy of Fine Arts in Madrid at family's wishes. Frequent visits to Prado Museum. Lives successively at San Pedro Mártir, 5 and in Jesús María and Lavapiés.
1898	*June*	Ill with scarlet fever. Returns to Barcelona.
	End June	Invited to l'Horta de Sant Joan (Terra Alta) by La Llotja friend Manuel Pallarès.

Picasso at the age of seven
with his sister Lola.
ACHB-AF

MAN WITH HAT

Signed P. Ruiz and dated 95 top right (La Coruña)
Oil on canvas
50.5 x 36
Donated by the artist, 1970
MPB 110.058

Between 1891 and 1895 the Ruiz-Picasso family lived in La Coruña. The move from the Mediterranean city of Picasso's birth, Malaga, to the Atlantic coast was motivated by financial reasons. Picasso's father taught drawing and ornamentation at the School of Fine Arts, which was in the same building as the La Guarda Institute where his son was studying. This coincidence was advantageous to the young Picasso who enrolled at the school where his father taught in September 1892 and studied both the normal curriculum and art.

The work of this period falls into two clearly stages. The first, from arrival in La Coruña to well into 1893, is markedly childish in character. The second, from 1983 to the departure for Malaga in the summer of 1895 reflected a maturity with a notable line and a good use of the different technical resources, which advances had been achieved thanks to his academic training.

1895 saw an intensification of works in oil. *Man in Hat* belongs to this year. It is one of the first in which he used a slightly larger format than usual.

In this sober, dense portrait, we observe the effort of the 14-year-old boy to move from an art that was predominantly aesthetic to one that was more expressive and human. He probably painted it having been stimulated by a propitious environment, rustic and verist, which gave him the chance to experience new sensations. The canvas falls within a freer and more intuitive tendency, pursued by Picasso parallel to another more formalist line represented by the academic works. Both lines of work are constant in his formative periods.

21

Portrait of the Artist's Mother

Signed *P. Ruiz Picasso* and dated *96* in *conté* pencil, bottom left
Pastel on paper
49.8 x 39 cm
Donated by the artist, 1970
MPB 110.016

In 1896 Picasso stepped up his activity as a portrait painter. He concentrated above all on his family surroundings. Father, mother, and sister came to sit regularly for the young artist and star in a significant number of paintings and drawings in which one can see the searching effort to capture the human being.

Of these works one of the most handsome is the portrait of his mother, María Picasso López (1855-1938), to whom Picasso bore a great physical resemblance and was always very close. He did not take long to make his mother's surname prevail, eventually using it as his only one in most of his works.

Like most of his juvenile drawings, this work follows the currents of the sensibility of its time and the aesthetic notions that guided him throughout these years of academic training. Picasso painted it before undertaking his own process of reflection, which led him to reconsider the established aesthetic values.

The technique of drawing, more subtle and bodily than that of painting, served him to give the figure of his mother a more fiery perception and one with more presence. It captures the moment when María, in profile, rests half asleep, her head tilting slightly forward and her eyes closed, in the new family home in carrer de la Mercè. The placid atmosphere married with the good use of drawing techniques, especially in the light reflections of the woman's face and in the texture of the cloth of the white blouse highlighted by lines of an icy white, make this a major work from the young Picasso's formative years.

Like Leonardo, Picasso believed that great love was born from the deepest knowledge of the "thing" that is loved. What one does not know, one cannot love, or at any rate loves it very meagrely.

23

PORTRAIT OF THE ARTIST'S FATHER

Unsigned, undated (Barcelona, *circa* 1896).
Water colour on paper
18 x 11.8 cm
Donated by the artist, 1970
MPB 110.281

José Ruiz Blasco (1838-1913), a master at the School of Fine Arts and painter, was one of the young Picasso's favourite models until 1899. During these formative years of the artist, the relationship between father and son was very close. José encouraged his son's vocation and watched over his every step in the field of art during Pablo's childhood and youth, deeply marking his entire learning process.

In fact, Picasso's father's personality left an indelible mark. As he confessed to Brassaï in 1943: "Every time I draw a man, I think, without meaning to, of my father (...). For me, the man is *don* José and will be all my life".

While visiting an exhibition of children's drawings in 1946, Picasso exclaimed: "In my childhood I could never have taken part in an exhibition like this: when I was twelve I drew like Raphael." He

was fifteen when he drew this splendid portrait of his father which highlights the mastery he had gained of the technique of drawing. The assured, unfaltering, swift line done with water colour leaves no room for second thoughts or retouching. The blue gives a melancholy, elegiac air to the atmosphere, making this work a foretaste of chromatic reduction to which Picasso was to subject his work some years later.

THE BEACH AT LA BARCELONETA

Unsigned, undated (Barcelona, *circa* 1896).
Oil on canvas
24.4 x 34 cm
Donated by the artist, 1970
MPB 110.073

Exercises in landscape is the focus of a major part of the work done by Picasso in his formative years. He was influenced partly by the importance attained by the genre in the 19th century and, in particular, by the interest awakened in the city of his birth, Málaga, with the arrival of the Valencian painter Muñoz Degrain (1843-1924).

Throughout 1896, landscape was of capital importance in Picasso's work, and became a regular, vital practice. His centres of interest were the family setting, the old town and its environs. These included the popular neighbourhood of La Barceloneta, built in the second half of the19th century, where fishermen and workers concentrated.

In *The Beach at La Barceloneta*, the artist used the view of the coastline to carry out a splendid exercise in perspective. He made use of the water breaking onto the sand to draw a diagonal that divides the composition. He used the two pictorial spaces for two different artistic styles: marked realism for the beach and associated elements (factories, horses...), and freer, more emotive brushwork, with notable blurring of the background for the sea and the horizon.

THE FIRST COMMUNION

■ Signed *P. Ruiz Picasso* and dated *1896* bottom right
Oil on canvas
118 x 166 cm
Donated by the artist, 1970
MPB 110.001

In September 1895 the Ruiz-Picasso family moved definitively to Barcelona, where José had obtained a teaching post the La Llotja School of Fine Arts. Pablo continued with the studies he had commenced in La Coruña. His two years at La Llotja consolidated his academic training.

Tutored by his father, he painted *The First Communion*, a canvas in a far more ambitious format than the one in which he usually worked. This served as his entrée to the official art world when he presented it to the Exhibition of Fine Arts and Artistic Industries of Barcelona. The event brought him his first major critique from the press: it was "the work of a new artist in which one discerns sentiment in the main characters and lines drawn with firmness".

The subject is totally conventional: the communion of his sister Lola. The girl is kneeling at the prie-dieu reading her missal. Her godfather bears a strong resemblance to her father, although he is very often identified as Dr Vilches, a friend of the family and father of Pedro, the choirboy in the presbytery who is putting a bunch of flowers on the altar. Picasso dedicated another oil to this boy, setting him in the presbytery putting out the candles in the candelabrum behind the flowers. The work, which belongs to the Montserrat Museum, links up with an oil here in the Picasso Museum: *A Choirboy Giving Oil to an Old Woman*, and its preliminary sketches.

The composition and the colouring of this work are totally academic. It was preceded by some preliminary drawings. All of these, as well as the set of drawings and paintings on ecclesiastic subjects that Picasso produced around the same time, many of which are here in the Museum, show that religious art was potentially profitable in the artistic environment in which he moved.

Picasso painted the canvas at the studio, at Plaça Universitat 5, of José Garnelo Alda (1866-1944), a teacher, friend and colleague of his father, and painter specialising in sacred and moralizing subjects. Three years before Garnelo had painted *Figure*, a girl dressed for first communion, seated, with a missal in her hands.

AUNT PEPA

Signed *P. Ruiz Picasso*. Undated (Málaga, summer 1896)
Oil on canvas
57.5 x 50.5 cm
Donated by the artist, 1970
MPB 110.010

Like every other year, in the summer of 1896 Picasso went with his family to Malaga, where he continued with his artistic exercises. The perseverance he had displayed in mastering the portrait resulted in one of the supreme works of his youth, the portrait of Josefa Ruiz Blasco (1825-1901), Aunt Pepa. He had already drawn her, sitting in an armchair, the previous summer in a album of drawings made in Málaga and Barcelona. In fact, it was then that Uncle Salvador, Josefa's brother, commissioned him to do the portrait, but Josefa's refusal and the young Picasso's reluctance delayed the project for a year.

The singularity of Aunt Pepa, a devout, solitary lady, is well reflected in this psychological portrait. Picasso captures the energetic nature, arrogant mien and extravagant personality of the old lady. The brushwork achieves an independence, a power and a value in itself never attained until now. The treatment of the light, with all the light concentrated on the face, which stands out violently and leaves the rest of the body and the background totally dark, links the work with baroque tenebrism. The legend spread by Sabartés, according to which the portrait was executed in less than an hour, lends even more merit to the work, if this is possible.

Mountain Landscape

Signed *P. Ruiz Picasso* and dated *Málaga* bottom right (summer 1896)
Oil on canvas
60.7 x 82.5cm
Donated by the artist, 1970
MPB 110.008

Over the summers of 1896 and 1897, landscape came to have a great importance in Picasso's work. Descriptions and analysis of sequences succeeded each other and in some cases served as the starting point for others.

The family's stay at the property of Pablo's godparents, the Blasco Alarcóns, at Llanes, gave him the chance to make an exhaustive study of the mountains of Málaga and its environs.

Mountain Landscape is the most important work of this period. It was preceded by preliminary studies, an oil and two panels. The thick, pastose brushwork together with the absence of line which is replaced by a combination of strokes in bright colours and an intense luminosity, marks Picasso's initial distancing from academic teachings. This was a serious attempt to reaffirm his personality.

By now he had felt the impact of the vision of light and colour of a group of Catalan artists who had left La Llotja bored with the stagnating canons taught there, precisely the same year that he had enrolled, It was the Saffron Group (Nonell, Mir, Canals, Pichot, Gual and Vallmitjana). Picasso had seen works of theirs at the Exhibition of Fine Arts and Artistic Industries of 1896 in which he took part with *The First Communion*.

SCIENCE AND CHARITY

Signed *P. Ruiz Picasso* bottom left. Undated (Barcelona, 1897)
Oil on canvas
197 x 249.5 cm
Donated by the artist, 1970
MPB 110.046

In 1897, Picasso had his first studio at Carrer de la Plata, 4. His father rented it to him for several days to enable him to paint *Science and Charity*, a large format composition that he presented at the National Fine Arts Exhibition in Madrid. In the registration details of this work he appears as a pupil of Muñoz Degrain, the teacher, old colleague and friend of his father then living in Madrid. Picasso was thus able to forge a link with the official world of academicist art.

This oil may be situated within the realist current. The title conveys two canons greatly in vogue in the late 19th century: philanthropic sentiments and the growing interest in the evolution of medical science. Both focussed on the sick woman who is the principal of the scene. This subject, which has a predecessor in Picasso's La Coruña phase, is a regular one in some consummate artists of the time such as Martínez de la Vega, a friend of Picasso's father, or Paternina.

This oil is preceded by seven sketches —five of them here in the Museum— and various notes. The scene takes place in a modest room where the sick woman lies on the bed, attended by a doctor, personified by José Ruiz. The woman was a beggar he had found in the street begging with her son and hired for 10 pesetas. The child lies in the arms of a nun who offers a cup to the sick woman and wears a habit of the community of Sant Vicenç de Paül lent by a friend of Uncle Salvador, Sister Josefa González.

The characters and the space are structured within rigorous classical canons. The colour that held sway at that time also bears the aftertaste of the classes Picasso was still receiving. The violet and ochre tones in some areas of the composition already denote a shift towards a kind of art in the air of the Barcelona of the time which was soon to prevail in his work.

After the Madrid exhibition, at which he obtained an honorable mention, Picasso presented the canvas at the Provincial Exhibition of Fine Arts in Málaga, where he was awarded the gold medal.

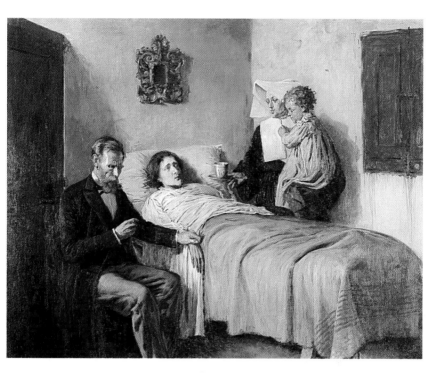

SELF-PORTRAIT WITH WIG

Unsigned and undated (Barcelona, *circa* 1897)
Oil on canvas
55.8 x 46 cm
Donated by the artist, 1970
MPB 110.053

Paraphrasing Leonardo da Vinci, Picasso once said: "The painter always paints himself." In the course of 1896 and 1897 he painted a series of self-portraits as an exercise in the continuous quest for a personal style. He treats his own image in very different ways. On this occasion his chameleon-like capacity led him to wear period costume, with 18th century clothes and wig.

Displaying fine irony and an undeniable sense of humour, he shows himself as a man of the court. The merit of the work lies in the exceptional technical mastery of the teenage artist. The vigorous brushwork and virtuoso treatment of the impasto lift it right away from the work of his fellow students and suggest a yearning for artistic liberation.

Although Picasso later told Brassaï "I never bothered much about my face", the truth is that throughout his life he painted a large number of self-portraits in which his figure takes on diverse personalities: courtier, sculptor, painter, bullfighter...

QUIQUET'S FARMHOUSE

Unsigned and undated (L'Horta de Sant Joan, 1898)
Oil on canvas
27 x 40 cm
Donated by the artist, 1970
MPB 110.066

In June 1898 Picasso was invited to L'Horta de Sant Joan by his friend and Llotja fellow student Manuel Pallarès (1876-1974). His stay was prolonged until January 1899 when he returned to Barcelona.

The study of the rural environment in all its facets and of the landscape he carried out then resulted in a set of drawings and paintings most of which are in the Museum. They are very fine works thanks to their marked naturalism. Their directness, spontaneity and luminosity make them a landmark in the evolution of Picasso's art.

Direct contact with nature furthered the emergence in his works of naturalism in both theme and colour which displays a total freedom of line and brushwork. This is the definitive move away from the strict academic rules.

The warm, fresh ambience that pervades Quiquet's farmhouse, together with the application of a new colouring and radiant light, make comprehensible what Picasso affirmed years later when he said that everything he knew he had learnt in Manuel Pallarès's town.

The intricate structure of the farmhouse, with a geometry that is highly complex, stimulated the creative capacity of the young artist and allowed him to play with areas of bright light and shade. At the same time he was able to practice perspective, over which he attained absolute mastery.

33

Contact with the Catalan Avant-Garde: 1899-1900

■

1899	*January*	Returns to Barcelona. Shares studio at carrer dels Escudellers Blancs, 2, with Santiago Cardona. Frequents Els Quatre Gats where he meets Carles Casagemas. Meets Jaume Sabartés
1900	*January*	Moves to studio at Riera de Sant Joan, 17, sharing with Carles Casagemas.
	February	First solo exhibition in the large room of Els Quatre Gats.
	July	Second exhibition at Els Quatre Gats.

Pablo Picasso, Mateu Fernández de Soto and Casagemas on the roof of number 3, carrer de la Mercé. AHCB-AF.

LOLA, THE ARTIST'S SISTER

Signed *P. Ruiz Picasso* top left. Undated (Barcelona, *circa* 1899)
Charcoal and crayon on paper
45 x 29.5 cm
Plandiura acquisition 1932
MPB 4.265

Lola (1884-1958), the second child of the Ruiz-Picassos, was the artist's regular model during his formative period.

This portrait is linked with a series of works produced between January 1899, when Picasso returned from L'Horta de Sant Joan, and the early months of 1900.

Picasso's output of this period displays the modernist spirit. Then, once again, drawing held a preeminent place in his work. The design of the female figure is delicate, although Picasso worked it with a firm, vigorous line which demonstrates his absolute mastery of the technique of drawing. The prevalence of undulation in the form belongs fully to *fin de siècle* aesthetics.

It was in this period that Picasso forged closer links with Catalan modernism. Enterprising and eager to find new avenues of plastic expression, he immediately tuned into the ideas that held sway in the artistic and intellectual circles of Barcelona. At that time, he

frequented the Els Quatre Gats brasserie. Promoted by Ramon Casas, Santiago Rusiñol and Miquel Utrillo, and with Pere Romeu as manager, it opened to the public on 12 June 1897. Until its closure in 1903, it was home to Barcelona's artistic and literary avant-garde.

THE COUCH

Signed *P. Ruiz Picasso* bottom right. Undated (Barcelona, 1899-1900)
Charcoal, pastel and crayon on varnished paper
26.2 x 29.7 cm
Plandiura acquisition, 1932
MPB 4.267

One of Picasso's most characteristic features was his great gift of observation. Nothing escaped the inquisitive gaze and the storehouse
of his great visual memory. His nightime outings to the cafés and
strolls through the typical streets of Barcelona of the late 19th century where the anarchist concerns were in the air more powerfully
than ever, provided him with a vast arsenal of images.

The Couch represents one of many everyday scenes in the dives
and taverns of Barcelona lowlife at the end of the 19th century.

The centre of the composition is a couple in a loving attitude seated on a couch. But what really creates dramatic tension and accentuates the expressionism of the scene is the old inquisitive-looking
bawd at the back left. Picasso takes a look at one of the central characters in the Spanish literary tradition, *La Celestina*, whom we already find in some drawings of 1897-1898 and, later, of 1901 in the
Museum. In 1968 he made a set of prints dedicated to La Celestina
which belong to the *347 prints* series.

Fascinated by the characters that emerge from everyday life, Picasso analysed their setting and applied it to his expressive needs. In
this composition, he uses objects which he outlines insistently with
a firm line. The table is made independent and marks a foreground
which fragments the figures, which are edged with a more ductile,
modelled line. The earthy colours that dominate the drawing unify

the scene. The work, still im-
bued with the autochthonous
expressionism of the Catalan
painter Nonell, was a prelude to
the drawings Picasso would
soon be making in Paris.

PORTRAIT OF THE WRITER RAMON REVENTÓS

Signed *P. Ruiz Picasso* at bottom. Undated (Barcelona, 1899-1900)
Water colour and charcoal on paper
66.5 x 30.1 cm
Donated by the artist, 1970
MPB 110.872

In February 1900, in the large exhibition room of the well-known Barcelona brasserie Els Quatre Gats, Picasso had his first one-man exhibition. This brought together a large group of portraits of his friends and Quatre Gats regulars. Picasso thus tried to make a place for himself within this artistic genre alongside Ramon Casas, the official portrait painter of the Catalan bourgeoisie.

The person portrayed here is Ramon Reventós (1881-1924), one of the regulars at Els Quatre Gats. He soon became one of the representatives of the avantgarde literature of the time. Attracted by journalism and gifted with a great sense of humour, he became a regular contributor to magazines such as *Catalunya Artística, Pèl*

& Ploma, Picarol... A great friend of Picasso, years later in 1947, he paid tribute to him by printing the two series of illustrations for the stories *El centaure picador* and *El capvespre d'un faune.*

Picasso probably drew this portrait of his friend Reventós between the end of 1899 and January 1900. The firm, assured line free of hesitation or indecision again displays the mastery of the technique achieved by the young artist and also his knowledge of artists like Toulouse-Lautrec and Steinlen.

DECADENT POET

Unsigned and undated (Barcelona, 1900)
Water colour and charcoal on paper
48 x 32 cm
Sabartés Collection 1970
MPB 70.232

Some months after Picasso met the sculptor and writer Jaume Sabartés (1881-1968), he painted two water colour portraits. Sabartés was a regular at the informal gatherings at Els Quatre Gats and soon became one of Picasso's best friends. In 1935 he also became his private secretary.

As Sabartés recounts in the book *Picasso, retratos y recuerdos*, they met in 1899 at the apartment of the brother of the sculptor Cardona, in carrer dels Escudellers Blancs. Months later, in the summer of 1900, Picasso drew *Decadent Poet*. Dressed in a Whistleresque cloak and with a crown of roses on his head, he holds a fleur-de-lis: "Picasso holds out a brush and asks me to model for him: Take it with your fingers, as if it were a flower..." Sabartés recounts.

This portrait falls within the literary and artistic currents of the last years of "vuitcentisme" in Barcelona. They were years dominated by marked antirealism steeped in the doctrines from northern Europe which had such an impact on the Catalan modernists.

CARRER DE LA RIERA DE SANT JOAN, FROM THE WINDOW OF THE ARTIST'S STUDIO

Unsigned and undated (Barcelona, 1900)
Oil on wood
22.3 x 13.8 cm
Donated by the artist, 1970
MPB 110.213

At the beginning of the century Picasso moved into a studio in the street Riera de Sant Joan, which he shared with Carles Casagemas (1880-1901), a painter with literary ambitions who was acquainted with the modernist brasserie. Riera de Sant Joan, which no longer exists, , was a very narrow, winding alley but full of life.

In this small oil, Picasso gives us a view of the street from the window of his studio. The motif of the window and its equivalents, which emerged significantly in his work of a few months before, in Madrid, now reappeared and would be recurrent in subsequent periods. From the Renaissance on it has been a well-exploited pictorial device serving as an excuse to see, observe and analyse a portion of concrete space and to work on perspective.

We observe that the window, wide open, precipitates us into the alley, like the charcoal of the same period also in the Museum. The prevailing scene is the city view. The window, of which we see only the bottom right hand corner of the frame, is a sign that justifies the external space with respect to the interior. It is a narrative and descriptive support through which the artist shows the daily life of this very busy place. The perspective, well elaborated, shapes the excellent composition of the work. The technique is meticulous as in the other small oils from the same period and once again reveals the sound training of the young artist.

The composition defines a substantial change in Picasso's pictorial composition, prompted by a turning towards abstraction and by the predominance of the patch of colour. The drawing work we see in the preceding works has disappeared. The brushwork is not at all conventional, on the contrary, it is excited and restless and accentuates even further the dynamism of the street.

Paris: 1900-1901

■

1900   *Just before*
            27 September   First trip to Paris, with Carles Casagemas
                                  Meets Pere Mañach, his first dealer. First contact
                                  with gallery owner Berthe Weill

            End December   Picasso and Casagemas return to Barcelona
            New Year   In Málaga, with Casagemas.

1901   *28 January*   Moves to Madrid.
            17 February   Casagemas commits suicide in Paris.
            March   Starts *Arte Joven* magazine with Francesc D'Assís Soler.
            1 to 16 June   Exhibition of Picasso and Ramon Casas at the Parés room,
                                  Barcelona, organised by the magazine *Pèl & Ploma*.
            June   Second trip to Paris, with Jaume Andreu Bonsoms.
            25 June-14 July   First solo exhibition in Paris at the Vollard Gallery.
                                  Meets poet Max Jacob.

THE EMBRACE

Signed *P. Ruiz Picasso*, bottom left. Undated (Paris, 1900)
Pastel on paper
59 x 35 cm
Plandiura acquisition 1932
MPB 4.263

During their first stay in Paris, Picasso and Casagemas moved into Nonell's studio in the popular Montmartre neighbourhood for a few months. The atmosphere there was quite different from that of Barcelona. Life in Paris was more permissive, freer.

The motif of the embrace is of interest not only socially but in plastic terms too. Now Picasso began to exploit it powerfully, although there are precedents in his work as is shown by the modernist drawings made in Barcelona between 1899 and 1900, also in the Museum. He investigated the subject in a deliberate, reasoned manner. He did not want to be descriptive: on the contrary, he wanted to take part in it so that he developed a series of works with the embrace as motif. The closest predecessors are the Kiss of Rodin and that of Toulouse-

Lautrec and the embraces of Munch, although this pastel is a representation inherited directly from Steinlen's street scenes.

In the foreground, Picasso gives us a couple. They are ordinary people, workers who might well have been described by the analytical and realistic pen of the great French novelist Émile Zola —the Museum has a sketch of Zola done in the same year. The couple express their feelings while strolling. They are in love and kiss in the street, on a dark night. The bodies and faces blend through the embrace and the kiss. The arms and hands, devoid of anatomical references, wrap around the lovers. The expressionist deformation of the bodies is accentuated with the bright colours and marked contours of the figures. Everything happens as if the couple's space were isolated from the outside urban space of the background. The urban landscape here at the service of the motif: the public embrace.

In the Dressing Room

Signed *P. Ruiz Picasso* and dated Paris, 1900, bottom right.
Pastel on paper
48 x 53 cm
Plandiura acquisition 1932
MPB 4.275

At the end of October 1900 Picasso went to Paris for the first time. With him went his friend, the painter Carles Casagemas. His work *Last Moments* had been chosen to be shown at the Universal Exhibition in Paris.

Picasso's stay in Paris gave him the chance to make direct contect with avantgarde currents and the work of artists the likes of Cézanne, Toulouse-Lautrec, Bonnard and Van Gogh which was on show at that time in the art galleries. He was also able to develop his great gifts of observation of everything around him. In fact, what really fascinated him was the life of the city, the night resorts and the people who frequented these lively, crowded places.

He took from these places the cabaret artist of *The Dressing Room* while she was making up, before going on stage. This is a pastel in which the expression of feelings takes precedence over all else in terms of rules of composition, as in many of Steinlen's works. The exquisite use of colour, full of shading and blooming with great vividness, shows once again how the young Picasso had mastered his craft.

The subject of the woman looking at herself in the mirror or making up begins this year in Picasso's work and is kept in filigreeuntil until it bursts forth with extraordinary virulence between 1905 and 1906. The female body in all its facets attracted Picasso from very early on, becoming one of his favourite subjects.

45

The End of the Number

Signed *Picasso*, bottom right. Undated. (Paris, 1901)
Pastel on canvas
72 x 46 cm
Plandiura acquisition 1932
MPB 4.270

From very early on Picasso was entranced by the world of entertainment in general: a fascinating world filled with visual stimuli, challenges and an inexhaustible source of inspiration which offered him a a wealth of thematic and iconographic possibilities.

In 1901 in Paris, Picasso was more dazzled than ever by the world of partying and entertainment and allowed himself to be seduced by Bohemia, the cabarets and the decadent pleasure of the *belle époque.*

In *The End of the Number* he captured the *vedette*, probably Yvette Gilbert, while taking her bow at the end of her act at the Olympia. The actor acting or greeting the audience on stage has been and still is a regular subject in the world of the visual arts. But Picasso moves away from the tradition represented by painters like Watteau, Delacroix and Degas in which emotional, pictorial, poetic and symbolic aspects prevail. He comes closer to artists like Daumier and, above all, Toulouse-Lautrec, although he is bolder.

Picasso inherited his liking for spontaneity and night subjects largely from this artist whose often inconsiderate gaze fascinated him. Years later he was to say: "It was in Paris that I realised what a great painter Toulouse-Lautrec is." He voiced his admiration for the French artist in works like this one, applying smooth, flat colours and using the arabesque in the line that traces the contour of the figure with clarity and great powers of synthesis and, above all, with an airy play of the wrist. The painter from Albi had once said that the model is always dessicated while his women were alive. Picasso, like his predecessor, sublimely captures the moment and presents the music hall star in full activity.

Signed *Picasso*, bottom left. Undated. (Paris, 1901)
Oil on cardboard
69.5 x 57 cm
Plandiura acquisition 1932
MPB 4.271

In the summer of 1901, Picasso's dealer, Pere Mañach, a Catalan established in Paris, organised an exhibition with the assistance of the art critic Gustave Coquiot and the dealer Ambroise Vollard in the latter's gallery in the rue Lafitte. Picasso exhibited together with the Basque painter Franciso Iturrino from 25 June to 14 July.

The critics gave Picasso favourable reviews. In the *Revue Blanche*, Félicien Fagus highlighted the polychromy of the works shown and said: "Like all pure painters, Picasso adores colour in itself." The exhibition made him known artistically and gave him the chance to make new contacts, the most significant being the poet Max Jacob who became one of his great friends. Jacob introduced Picasso to the avantgarde literary circles and to reading that pushed him towards new avenues of plastic expression.

The works shown at the Vollard gallery were basically portraits, street scenes, music hall interiors... They are markedly expressionist, along the lines of Steinlen, Toulouse-Lautrec and Munch. They evince a search for the exaltation of colour over and above all, together with the practice of a loose, separate brushstrokes. The bold colouring moved Daix to speak of pre-

Fauvism, a style that other contemporary artists such as Marquet and Matisse were also experimenting with.

This oil is probably *The Morphine Addict* that figures in the catalogue of the Vollard gallery exhibition. It is interesting to see how here Picasso felt captivated by a Goyaesque play of natural and artificial light and how he has fun with the use of colour. For example, through red he expresses things as different as painted lips, the hat, the dress, finally splashing the wall in the background.

THE DWARF

Signed *Picasso*, bottom left. Undated. (Paris, 1901)
Oil on cardboard
102 x 60 cm
Plandiura acquisition 1932
MPB 4.274

The echo of Goya's phrase "Ugliness is beauty" reaches this magnificent oil painted in Paris in 1901. Once again, the worldly, night theme invades the creative world of the artist, although now he recalls a classical theme in Spanish painting, physical deformation as a motif for creation, previously used by Velázquez and Goya, amongst others. But unlike his masters, Picasso does not turn the dwarf's deformity into a spectacle: in fact in this case the defect is anecdotal, and in the light of the lamps - like the dancers of Degas or the *Jane Avril* of Toulouse-Lautrec- shows a woman with an inquisitive, non complacent and above all provocative gaze.

The painting gives off great energy and originality, thanks basically to the virtuosity in the colouring.

Picasso uses a light, loose brushstroke, called macrodivisionism by Lafuente Ferrari, which in some places gives the work the texture of a mosaic. There is little drawing in this oil. The energetic polychromy of this period soon gives way to a reduction of colour without precedent in Picasso work.

STILL LIFE

Signed *Picasso*, bottom left. Undated. (Paris, 1901)
Oil on canvas
59 x 78 cm
Plandiura acquisition 1932
MPB 4.273

In April 1902 Picasso exhibited at the Berthe Weill gallery in Paris. *Still Life* is the work that figures in the catalogue of the exhibition as number 1, to which Adrien Fargue referred in the preface saying: "Sometimes he gets carried away by colour, and then he gives us this luxuriant still life."

Picasso had painted the oil one year before in Paris, and it was his first ambitious work on the subject. To do it he used what the painter Denis had defined years before as a "group of colours brought together with a certain order", which is the reality of any painting.

The composition evokes a sumptuous meal in which the pleasures of gastronomic refinement have delighted an anonymous diner. The sea food —empty oyster shells with pastose brushwork and delicate colour— the products of the earth —fruit with bright and in some cases Cézanne-style colours— and also the flowers —a bunch with no perspective like the ones done by Matisse— rest on hand-made ceramic supports: it is worth recalling here that in the late forties Picasso was to become an extraordinary ceramist. On the right is a typical beer mug from the region of Quimper, where his great friend the poet Max Jacob was born.

Picasso models the forms of objects with skilful outlining using vigorous, pastose and imprecise brushstrokes. The painting has a luminous appearance. Picasso's passion for colour is perfectly obvious here, where he energises the ensemble by the indulgent confrontation of yellow, orange and red on a cold blue background and the icy white tablecloth. In spite of the vivid colouring overall, blue dominates the atmosphere and heralds the move towards monochrome that would soon invade Picasso's works.

50

The Blue Period: 1901-1904

1901	*Autumn*	Beginning of the blue period.
1902	*January*	Returns to Barcelona. Shares studio at Nou de la Rambla 10, with Angle Fernández de Soto and Josep Rocarol. Returns to Els Quatre Gats and also frequents El Guayaba.
	1-15 April	Joint exhibition with Louis Bernard Lemarie at the Berthe Weill Gallery in Paris.
	19 October *15 November-* *15 December*	Departure for Paris with Josep Rocarol. Exhibition Picasso, Pichot, Girieud and Launai at the Berthe Weill gallery.
1903	*Mid-January*	Return to Barcelona. Shares studio at Riera de Sant Joan, 17, with Angel Fernández de Soto.
1904	*January* *12 April*	Moves to studio at Comerç, 28. Fourth and definitive trip to Paris. With Sebastià Junyer Vidal. Moves into the building known as the Bateau Lavoir, rue de Ravignan, 13.

Pablo Picasso in the Place Ravignan in 1904. © Photo R.M.N.

THE WOMAN WITH THE CAP

Signed *Picasso*, top left. Undated (Paris, 1901)
Oil on canvas
41 x 33 cm
Jacqueline Picasso donation, 1985
MPB 112.750

In the spring of 1901 Picasso made a second trip to Paris, where he lived until the following January. He took the studio that a few months before had been occupied by the ill-fated Carles Casagemas. Picasso then produced a series of works in memory of his friend that mark the transition to the blue period. Between the autumn of that year and January of the next, his work underwent a radical change in both colour and subject matter. Some time later he said that he started to paint in blue when thinking about the death of his friend.

In late summer or early autumn Picasso visited the women's prison of Sainte-Lazare in Paris, obtaining a pass thanks to Dr Julien. The result of his visits was a set of works focussing on the inmates, mostly prostitutes suffering from venereal diseases. Throughout his life Picasso was fascinated by the taboo characters who star in supremely important works like *Les Demoiselles d'Avignon*.

The Woman with the Cap belongs to this group of prisoners, victims of society, whom Picasso removed from the sinister vaulted corridors of the prison and set against curtains or neutral grounds. These form an undefined timeless space like a limbo ("blue limbo"). The decontextualisation of the figures turns the sick woman, despairing and ill-treated by life, into a woman who evinces tremendous sensibility and serenity.

Stylistically, the figure, outlined in black, links up with the stylisation and mannerism of El Greco and with the simplification of Gauguin, with whom he also shares the plastic use of the decorous headgear, the Phrygian cap in this case- the Breton cap in Gauguin. The white cap was worn by syphilis sufferers. The inmates' uniform, as well as the singular cap, consisted of a baggy black-and-white striped blouse, which Picasso usually replaced with a blue habit, clearly influenced by El Greco.

This figure greatly resembles the woman who appeared in an x-ray examination of the *Blue Portrait of Jaume Sabartés* of 1901, also in the Museum.

SEATED WOMAN

Signed *Picasso/A*. Undated (Barcelona, 1902)
Bronze
14 x 11 x 8 cm
Sabartés Collection
MPB 70.244

From January to 19 October 1902, the day he left again for Paris, Picasso lived in Barcelona. He frequented the same avantgarde milieus as previously. From the artistic point of view he was now he totally immersed in the first style that was personal and entirely his own, known as the blue period.

Some months after his arrival he made his first sculpture, the only one in this Museum, Seated Woman. It is an individual piece, like most of the sculptures he was to produce, and modest in size, an occasional work executed in the studio of his good friend the sculptor Emili Fontbona, in the summer residence of his family in the city's Sant Gervasi neighbourhood.

The work is undeniably religious and symbolic in character. Iconographically, this female figure is well represented in the painting and drawing of the period: a woman dressed in long robes, dejected and abandoned to her own burden. Here, Picasso transferred a theme from his painting to the three-dimensional plastic medium. He had no difficulty in finding a solution and sat her on a block, which he modelled greatly simplifying the facial traits, as in some pictorial works of 1902, and also the arms and legs, which he only hints at.

Cirici finds certain coincidences between these figures of Picasso and those of the Catalan Romanesque murals. Apparently, on one occasion, contemplating the frescoes of Santa Maria de Tahull, Picasso said: "Look, I did that."

ROOFS OF BARCELONA

Unsigned and undated (Barcelona, 1902)
Oil on canvas
57.8 x 60.3 cm
Donated by the artist, 1970
MPB 110.020

As we have seen, the urban landscape attracted Picasso from very early on. When he arrived in Barcelona in January 1902 he moved into the studio at number 10, Nou de la Rambla, which was rented by two friends of his, Angel Fernández de Soto, known as "El Patas", and Rocarol. Impelled by curiosity, Picasso explored his new surroundings exhaustively. One result was this oil of the roofs of the city which displays immense resourcefulness in its composition.

Picasso was captivated by the amalgam of structures visible from the roof of the new studio. As a result, he offered an urban view ela-

borated with a structure of linear planes floating in a melancholy, forming an exquisite architectural reading of the surroundings.

This twilight scene embodies a new vision of the volumes which turn the composition into a delicious study of forms which are facilitated by means of colour and accentuated by the good use of the contrasts between sun and shade which give more projection to the perspective.

This canvas was used several times. X-ray photography has shown that it had previously been painted with a male bust in profile. On the back is a rural landscape with mountains in the background.

THE BLUE GLASS

Unsigned and undated (Barcelona, 1902-1903)
Oil on canvas
66.1 x 28.5 cm
Donated by the artist, 1970
MPB 110.009

Simplicity of composition and technical mastery make this small oil a work of exceptional plastic beauty.

Picasso turns a simple glass into a vase containing a flower. He once said: "The most ordinary object is a vessel, a vehicle for my thought. It is for me what a parable was for Christ." The glass is taken from the café and cabaret scenes of the Barcelona and Paris of the time which abound in his work, from the tables on which his dejected characters or friends lean, and is individualised on another table where it shares the limelight with a flower with red petals.

The sparkle of the glass is brought out with white and touches of dark blue which gives it the total transparency and immateriality which accentuate the mysterious, symbolic tone of the work. Through it, the view is prolonged as far as the opaque blue wall of the background. This colour tints the entire composition with the exception of the red petals of the flower, the heart and nerves of which are blue. We have already seen this type of amaryllis lily, a symbol of *fin de siècle* decadence: in the hand of Jaume Sabartés in *Decadent Poet*, in some drawings of that time in the Museum, and in the bouquet in the *Still Life* of 1901.

An x-ray study has revealed a painting of a man in profile beneath this work.

The Woman with the Lock of Hair

Signed *Picasso* and dated *1903* top left (Barcelona, 1903)
Water colour on paper
50 x 37 cm
Plandiura Acquisition, 1932
MPB 4.268

In January 1903 Picasso returned to Barcelona and set up in the studio rented by his friend Angel Fernández de Soto, at number 17, Riera de Sant Joan: the same one he had shared three years before with Carles Casagemas.

It is highly likely that he arrived in time to see the collective exhibition at the Parés gallery with works by Isidre Nonell, the Catalan painter who best depicted the world of marginalisation, in as embodied in particular in the gypsy women the outlying areas of turn-of-the-century Barcelona.

Sometimes Picasso's characters, like the woman in this drawing, do not represent an indictment of social injustice in the world. They simply present a vision of people from marginalised social groups, with an almost poetical meaning.

Picasso removed the girl from her habitat and, as we have seen him do with other figures, placed her in a neutral framework. Once

again he immersed the character in the empty setting of poverty which he tints blue. A narcotic effect is achieved with the ubiquitousness of this colour which imbues the background and also invades the bust, and which may link up perfectly with the portraits of gypsies painted by Nonell. The figure is outlined with black pastel, which gives it more relief. The face is undaunted, serene and compliant. The large black eyes are lifeless and the gaze, lost on the horizon, reflects the indifference of one who has nothing and has lost all hope.

THE FORSAKEN

Signed and dated *Picasso 1903*, top right (Barcelona)
Pastel and charcoal on paper
46 x 40 cm
Plandiura Acquistion, 1932
MPB 4.269

The mother and child was a regular subject in Picasso's work between 1901 and 1905. These paintings show the influence of the French painter and theorist Maurice Denis, and also the painter Puvis de Chavannes —one of the artists whose work most influenced Picasso during this period—, both of whom were widely reported in the magazines of late 19th and early 20th century Barcelona.

Like the rest of the figures, Picasso's mother and child paintings of the period show the heavy charge of personal, environmental, social and cultural factors discharged therein by the artist without compunction. At that time he was convinced that art emanated from sadness and pain, and that pain was at the heart of life.

In *The Forsaken*, Picasso focused the drawing on the busts of the

mother and child, who take up almost the entire composition against a neutral ground bathed in blue softened with ochre tones.

Like many female figures of the period, the woman is shrouded in a brown cloak with which she swathes her child —there is a pen drawing of the child in the Museum. With her hand, which is disproportionately large thanks to the El Greco type mannerisms displayed by some of Picasso's figures, she shields it from the rigours of the winter.

The flesh colour of the figures has been humanised again. The technical execution shows great virtuosity, especially because it attains an excellent luminosity thanks to the application of touches of white pastel. This vivacity of the flesh contrasts with the inexpressiveness of the faces; what stands out is the moving gaze of the round black eyes filled with the indifference and resignation that pervades the world of the marginalised.

PORTRAIT OF SEBASTIÀ JUNYENT

Unsigned and undated (Barcelona, circa 1903)
Oil on canvas
73 x 60 cm
Donated by the artist, 1970
MPB 110.018

Picasso's stay in Barcelona from mid January 1903 to 12 April 1904, when he moved definitively to Paris, was his most prolific time in terms of portrait production within the blue period.

One of the finest portraits was dedicated to his friend Sebastià Junyent i Sans (1865-1908) with whom he then had increasingly close ties. A painter, illustrator and graphic designer, Junyent was also an essayist and art critic for important magazines such as *Joventut* and *La Renaixença*, who gave him deserved prestige.

Financially well-to-do thanks to an inheritance from his uncle of the same name, Junyent helped Picasso more than once and even suggested he share his studio in the Carrer Bonavista in the Gràcia neighbourhood. There, they painted a portrait of each other. Junyent's has as its background *Life*, which Picasso was painting at that time, and which Junyent bought together with *The Old Jew* for five hundred pesetas. Thanks to his comfortable position, he became a good collector of Picasso, although later the works were scattered.

The *Portrait of Sebastià Junyent* is of great plastic beauty. Picasso

reddened the face to give it a natural tone which he had done away with in most of the figures of this period. The execution of the hair displays great technical subtlety. The contour of the figure is done with a thick black outline which splashes and trickles on part of the background. The blue used by Picasso is softer than some time before, it is a "Barcelona blue".

THE MADMAN

■ Signed *Picasso* and dated *1904* top left
Water colour on paper
85 x 35 cm
Sebastià Junyent Collection. Plandiura Acquisition 1932
MPB 4.272

The formal mutations of Picasso's figures of this period seem to find one of their maximum exponents in *The Madman*, a capital drawing of this period.

Stylistically, the character links up with the beggars, the old and the blind that Picasso painted and drew insistently throughout 1903 and 1904, and connects fully with a water colour with the same title he painted the same year.

The Madman is taken directly from human wretchedness, executed by Picasso with sublime skill. He made use of a technique of El Greco, the great 16th-century master whom he had admired for years. The oil *Portrait of An Unknown in the Style of El Greco* and the drawings and caricatures of El Greco's figures, all of 1899 in our Museum are proof of this admiration.

The original, personal style of El Greco, which crystallised in a tendency to elongate his figures, sometimes to the point of denaturing them, is marked in this work by Picasso.His taste for mannerism, thanks to which the conventional axes of the composition are broken, establishing a rupture between function and form, is evident not only in the stylised body but also in the feet and hands. The latter, extremely disproportionate and skeletal, are distorted and come close to the face, where all the dramatic tension is focused thanks to its powerful expressionism, which makes quite clear the sickness of the unhappy wretch., Picasso once told Brassaï, referring to El Greco: "I had already seen some of his paintings, which I admired (...) I decided to make a trip to Toledo and they made a profound impression on me. If my figures of the blue period are stretched, it's probably because of his influence (...)".

The contours of the figure are done a vigorous line, with some parts underscored. The blue water colour softly tints some areas of the body and in some places goes beyond the limits of the human profile to lightly tint parts of the background and to simulate shadow on an undefined floor.

Picasso probably dedicated and gave the work to his good friend Sebastià Junyent in payment for for having sold *La Vida* for him some time before.

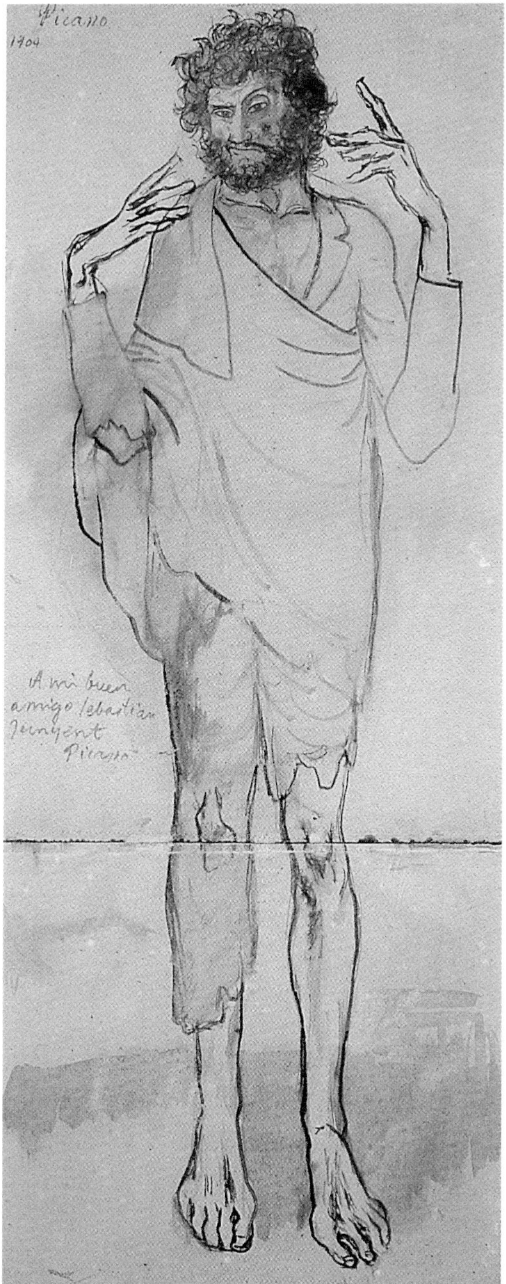
Picasso
1904
A mi buen
amigo Sebastian
Junyent
Picasso

From the Rose Period to 1916

■

1904	*Autumn*	Meets Fernande Olivier (1881-1966), his partner until spring 1912

Fernande Olivier, Pablo Picasso and Ramon Reventós at the Guayabo, c. 1904. AHCB-AF

1905	*Early autumn*	Beginning of Rose Period. Meets Leo and Gertrude Stein.
1906	*Spring between 22 and 29 May mid-August*	Meets Henri Matisse Arrives in Gòsol (Alt Berguedà) Returns to Paris
1907	*Spring March-July Summer*	Meets Braque Paints *Les demoiselles d'Avignon.* Meets Daniel-Henri Kahnweiler, his second dealer.
1908	*Summer 14 November*	Stays in La-Rue-des-Bois (Oise), town near Paris Review by Louis Vauxelles in *Gil Blas* in connection with the Braque exhibition at the Kahnweiler gallery, in which he coined name for the new artistic style: Cubism.

1909	*Beginning May*	Moves to Barcelona with Fernande.
	5 June–	
	early September	L'Horta de Sant Joan.

Pablo Picasso in Horta de Sant Joan, 1909.
© *Photo R.M.N.*

1910	*1 July-26 August*	Cadaqués (Alt Empordà).
	August	Several days in Barcelona with Fernande, André Derain and the latter's partner Alice.

1911	*5 July-5 September*	Ceret (Vallespir) with Manolo Hugué and Braque.
	Autumn	Meets Eva Gouel (Marcelle Humbert) (1885-1915).

1912	*Summer*	Ceret with Eva, short stay in Avignon (Provence).
		Back in Paris produces first collages and *assemblages*.

1913	*Spring-summer*	Ceret with Eva.
	3 June	Death of father. In Barcelona briefly for funeral.

1914	*Summer*	Avignon with Eva.

	2 August	Outbreak of World War I. Braque, Derain, Apollinaire... conscripted. Picasso spared from going to front by his Spanish nationality.
	November	Returns to Paris.
1915	*December*	Jean Cocteau and composer Edgar Varese visit him at his studio
	14 December	Eva dies of tuberculosis.
1916	*May*	Introduced by Jean Cocteau to Serge Diaghilev, director of the Russian Ballet, who asks him to work on the ballet *Parade*.

PORTRAIT OF MRS CANALS

Signed Picasso upper right. Undated (Paris, 1905)
Oil on canvas
88 x 68 cm
Plandiura Acquisition, 1932
MPB 4.266

In 1905 Picasso painted the splendid *Portrait of Mrs Canals*. Mrs Canals was the companion of the Catalan painter and engraver Ricard Canals (1876-1936) who was then living in Paris. Years later Fernande Olivier, Picasso's first companion, explained that Canals: " (...) is painting a picture for the exhibition. A box at a bullfight. Two Spanish women with shawl —one black (Bernadetta), the other white (me)— propped on our elbows, watching and laughing. The clothes are picturesque and have beautiful embroidered shawls, laid on the railing of the box (...)". From that oil, commissioned by the banker Ivo Bosch, emerged this exceptional portrait.

The beauty of Bernadetta Bianco (1870-1958), the Italian model who had inspired Degas and Bartholomé, had such an impact on Picasso that he dedicated this sober oil of marked classicism.to her. The figure is immersed in an ethereal atmosphere bathed in the iridescent pink tones typical of this new period of Picasso, which never attained the monochromatic intensity of the preceding one.

The artist focuses attention on the face of the Roman woman which he describes meticulously, highlighting her extraordinary beauty. He frames her with a black mantilla, with well evidenced edging, fixed in place with a comb and adorned with a mauve flower. Picasso's Bernadetta falls within the theme of Spanish women of the folklore tradition, very typical in the work of Canals and other artists of the time, which were very popular with the French public.

Picasso did this composition in his studio in the building popularly known as Bateau Lavoir, which he moved into in April 1904. It was a very odd building, inhabited by young poets and artists, located in Rue Ravignan in Montmartre. Close by was the Medrano circus which Picasso and his friends frequented. Soon the world of strolling players, acrobats and other circus characters took over Picasso's work and transformed his representative universe.

70

THE OFFERING

Signed *Picasso*. Undated (Paris, 1908)
Wash on paper
30.8 x 31.1 cm
Donated by Lord Amulree, 1985
MPB 112.761

In the spring of 1908 Picasso produced a series of studies on this work, and also another wash and a small oil. The set, which was probably a project for a larger work, is related to *Les Demoiselles d'Avignon*, the oil which displays a rupture between formal rhythms and space.

In this wash. Picasso returned to the theme of the nude woman viewed by a man —on this occasion by two— that he had already tackled in 1904. But now this became a regular motif in his work. We should recall that in the future he was to rework it to the point, at times, of obsession.

The theme of the recumbent nude woman observed by a man in *The Offering* brings us close to Cézanne in his new *Olympia* and *Afternoon in Naples*. The detail of the drapery held by the man on the right which hangs down and trails on the floor evokes the bathers of Cézanne.

Picasso's woman here departs from the model of traditional representation because her posture is simultaneously reclining and upright, an intentional contradiction which serves as an introduction to Cubism. First and foremost this represents the total decomposition of the elements, which have to be mentally reconstructed by the observer, who can view them from different angles at the same time.

Picasso's Olympia, like some of the women in Greek and Roman statuary or in the paintings of Ingres, Cézanne and their contemporary Matisse, lifts her arm behind her head, making a closed arch over the hair. This pose recurs in the female figures represented by Picasso in this period. In the drawing, as in other works, he endeavours to create the space by means of relations in the situation of the figures, darkening those in the foreground, the men, in order to lighten the woman in the background. He uses the opposite technique to that usually employed to create distance in classical perspective. The palette uses a rich range of ochres and Prussian blue, with black for modelling the figures with a thick line.

Between the Wars: 1917-1940

1917	*January*	Brief stay in Barcelona
	February	To Rome with Cocteau to work on *Parade* with the Russian Ballet. Meets ballerina Olga Kokhlova (1891-1955). Visits Naples, Pompeii and Florence.
	June-November	Barcelona.
		Returns to Paris. Lives in Montrouge with Olga.

Dinner in honour of Picasso at the Galeries Laietanes, 1917. AHCB-AF.

1918	*12 July*	Marries Olga in Paris.
	Summer	Biarritz (French Basque Country) at the home of Madame Errazuriz.
	8 November	Meets André Breton

| 1919 | | To London to join Ballets Russe. |
| | *August* | Saint Raphaël (Provence) |

| 1920 | | Continues close collaboration with Russian Ballet, which continues for some years. |
| | *Summer* | With Olga in Juan-les-Pins (Provence) |

1921	4 February	Birth of Paulo Picasso.
	Summer	Fontainebleau (Seine et Marne)
1922	Summer	Dinard (Brittany)
1923	Summer	Antibes (Provence)
1924	Summer	Juan-les-Pins
	October	Breton's *Manifeste du surréalisme* published.
1925	March-April	Montecarlo: coincides with Russian Ballet season.
	Summer	Juan-les-Pins
1926	Summer	Juan-les-Pins
	October	Brief stay in Barcelona
1927	January	Meets Marie-Thérèse Walter (1909-1977), with whom has relationship until 1936.
	Summer	Cannes with Olga and Paulo.
1928	May	Start of professional collaboration with sculptor Juli González.
	Summer	Dinard with Olga and Paulo, as following summer.
1930	June	Buys Boisgeloup Castle near Gisors (Normandy).
1931	May	Moves into castle, where also spends following summer. Works above all on sculpture.
	Summer	Juan-les-Pins
1933	1 June	First issue of *Minotaur* magazine, for which did cover.
1934	Summer	Holiday in Spain with Olga and Paulo. Pass through Barcelona.
1935	Spring	Break with Olga.
	5 September	Birth of Maya, to Marie-Thérèse Walter.
	12 September	Sabartés becomes Picasso's private secretary.
1936	March-May	Juan-les-Pins with Marie-Thérèse and Maya. Meets Dora Maar (1907-1997), a photographer with links with the Surrealist movement.
	18 July	Outbreak of Spanish Civil War.
	Autumn	Tremblay-sur-Mauldre with Marie-Thérèse and Maya.
	20 November	Appointed honorary director of the Prado Museum, Madrid.

1937	*26 April*	The town of Guernica (Basque Country) bombed by German air force.
	May-June	Works on *Guernica* in studio at Grands-Augustins, 7, Paris.
	Summer	Holiday at Mougins with Dora Maar and the Éluards, with whom he returns the following year.
1939	*13 January*	Death of María Picasso López in Barcelona.
	July-August	Antibes with Dora Maar at house of Man Ray.
	September	Settles in Royan with Dora Maar and Sabartés. Marie-Thérèse and Maya move nearby.
		Outbreak of World War II.
1943	*May*	Meets Françoise Gilot (1921), his partner for ten years.
1944	*5 October*	L'*Humanité* announces affiliation to French Communist Party.
1945		End of World War II.
	Summer	Cap d'Antibes with Dora Maar.
	Autumn	Intense activity in printmaking and close collaboration with printer Mourlot.

HARLEQUIN

Unsigned and undated (Barcelona, 1917)
Oil on canvas
116 x 90 cm
Donated by the artist, 1919
MPB 10.941

Picasso's links with the show business world are quite notorious in the works of his youth. But it was not until 1917 that he became directly involved. Thanks to the intrepid poet Jean Cocteau he made contact with the Russian Ballet directed by Serge Diaghilev, with whom he worked for several years. He went to Rome with Cocteau to work on the ballet *Parade* and to meet the company, which was touring Italy.

Picasso took advantage of the trip to see Naples and Pompeii and thus make direct contect with the classical civilisation of the Mediterranean. This approach to the classical sources resulted in the "return to order" and the consolidation of a period, known equally as classical and Ingresian, that had started to emerge timidly in 1914. *Harlequin* is one of the first major exponents of this approach. Traditional figuration returned to Picasso's world and coexisted with the cubist style which for years had almost monopolised his work.

Harlequin was one of the first canvases Picasso painted while he was in Barcelona from June to November 1917. It was preceded by some drawings, of which one, of a bust, belongs to the Museum.

The *Harlequin* is Léonide Massine (1896-1979), a privileged model of the period. The young Muscovite became the company's lead dancer, having been engaged by Diaghilev in the winter of 1913-1914 to replace Nijinksy. From 1917 he combined dancing with choreography. Picasso presents him on a stage with is a rail slightly covered with a bright red curtain contrasting with the earthy ochres of the flesh and the greens, blues and pinks of the typical diamond-patterned of the figurer, his *alter ego*. The harlequin is a figure well represented in Picasso's work of 1905, when the world of street performers and the circus burst into it obsessively. The earthy colour of the skin and the large, chubby hands, showing Picasso's interest in developing the volume of forms, stand at the vanguard of the monumental figures drawing on antiquity and Ingres, which were to reach their zenith between 1920 and 1923.

Two years after painting this magnificent oil, Picasso donated it to the Art Museums of Barcelona.

WOMAN WITH MANTILLA

Unsigned and undated (Barcelona, 1917)
Oil on canvas
89 x 116 cm
Donated by the artist, 1970
MPB 110.004

Richness of style and meticulous technique are fundamental features of the splendid portrait of the companion of Malagan painter Rafael Martínez Padilla (1878-1958).He was one of the group of friends, along with the artists Maeztu and Iturrino, who paid tribute to Picasso at the Galeries Laietanes during his stay in Barcelona in 1917. The oil is also known popularly as "La Salchichona" on account of the difficulty encountered by the young woman, of French origin, in pronouncing the Spanish word *salchichón* (a type of sausage).

The serenity and beauty of the model place her near the 1905 portrait of Mrs Canals. The composition is elegant and rigorous although the work is unfinished, a trait that the artist repeats on other occasions. The classical workmanship is close to Ingres and the pictorial method to the pointillism perfected by Seurat and Signac with their reworking of Impressionism in scientific terms.

The methodical application of pure colours with tiny brushstrokes

which blend and complement each other on the observer's retina, the purity of the line determining the lovely face of the woman, and the spontaneous and at the same time firm line that shapes the body, the comb and mantilla, make this composition a work of great virtuosity.

This oil is very similar to the one presented by Martínez Padilla himself at the 1919 Art Exhibition in Barcelona, entitled *The Mantilla*.

BLANQUITA SUÁREZ

Unsigned and undated (Barcelona, 1917)
Oil on canvas
73.3 x 47 cm
Donated by the artist, 1970
MPB 110.013

For Picasso, his stay in Barcelona represented meeting with his family and friends. The latter received him with triumphal honours, organised meetings and wrote articles about him in the magazines of the time such as *Vell i Nou*, *l'Esquella de la Torratxa*, etc., in which his works were also reproduced. Here, of particular significance was the review entitled "Banquete Picasso" which appeared in *La Publicitat* on 13 July, the day after the banquet put on by friends and acquaintants at the Lyon d'Or.

In Barcelona Picasso returned to his old haunts and watering places, as shown by this oil in which Blanquita Suárez, the comic soprano as she advertised herself, performs at the Tivoli Theatre. A few months before, starting on 20 January, the dancer had already given

ven some highly successful performances. When the theatre season was over, after some time away from the city, she returned to work on 28 June, which is when we believe Picasso to have seen her.

Once again, he put the figure at the centre of the show, on the stage, which he structures with sharp, arid geometric planes, where, thanks to a well thought out play of tones he creates a magnificent perspective. The figure also displays superimposed planes, although Picasso softened it by applying more modulated, curved lines to some parts of the body; in combination with the more angular ones, these create the sensation of movement, of dance. This is one of the most relevant features of this oil (in a block produced at the same time in Barcelona belonging to the Musée de Picasso of Paris, there are some sketches of a dancer dancing, probably Blanquita Suárez). The colours are saturated, with black, brown, green and white dominating, with violet touches in some places.

Picasso here achieves a rigorously constructed composition in which he successfully blends technical severity with the grace and spontaneity of the captured moment.

FIGURE WITH FRUIT BOWL

Unsigned and undated (Barcelona, 1917)
Oil on canvas
100 x 70.2 cm
Donated by the artist, 1970
MPB 110.006

The year 1917 represented the consolidation of the convergence of two styles in Picasso's work, the cubist and the naturalist. *Figure with Fruit Bowl* is a clear exponent of this, because the artist again includes figurative fragments, in this case the hand holding the knife and fork, in the composition of geometric rhythms.

The figure is close to the structures he used in those of 1915 and 1916, worked with great purity of form and with plain, cold colours which show some move towards abstraction, which in Picasso is always figurative.

In this work Picasso achieved a masterly composition, through meagre planes of mounting rhythm which define the body and culminate in the face, which he compensates with a grey square where he places the black eye. The arms, well defined and done with marked undulations, balance the composition. The left one, red and outlined with a thick, black line, contrasts with the chromatic severity of the work as a whole, from which the still life in the foreground also escapes. The superimposition of planes and the undulations that shape this figure are the same ones as used by Picasso used in *Woman In A Chair* and in particular *Man Seated* in the Museum's collection..

The white bowl filled with fruit displays a more nuanced structure of planes, which Picasso recreated in a small-format oil.

FRUIT BOWL

Unsigned and undated (Barcelona, 1917)
Oil on canvas
40 x 28.1 cm
Donated by the artist, 1970
MPB 110.029

Fruit Bowl is a motif from the oil *Figure with Fruit Bowl*, taken out by Picasso in order to devote an entire composition to it. The still life had interested him for years and he was to exploit it exhaustively, to the point where he can be said to be one of the artists who has most worked in this genre.

Stylistically, it is a handsome recapitulation of the cubist lessons which had dominated his work for some time, although it has lost the hermeticism of the preceding years and displays more sensual texture and colouring which make it more emotive. The fruit is given a more naturalistic treatment than the rest of the painting. Creamy tones dominate the composition, which is reinforced with greys and dirty whites contrasting in some places with blacks, reds, greens and whites.

PASSEIG DE COLOM

Unsigned and undated (Barcelona, 1917)
Oil on canvas
40.1 x 32 cm
Donated by the artist, 1970
MPB 110.028

Between 1901 and 1914, the motif of the window or equivalent appears to lose force in Picasso's work, giving way to a representation in which space and form interrelate within a framework of homogeneous texture which unifies all.

In Barcelona, Picasso tackled this subject afresh. He made a series of drawings and this oil from the balcony of the Pension Ranzini at Passeig de Colom, 22, close to his parents' home where he was living. At the luxurious pension was lodged the Russian Ballet, including Olga, his fiancée, whom he visited every day. She was soon to become his wife. The view from the pension rooms prompted him to work again, as he had years before, on the theme of the window or balcony, which eventually became become a regular practice.

In the foreground is a balcony which, through the railing, plunges us towards the street in a masterly exercise in perspective. On the iron railing, a gust of wind has moved the Spanish flag, which stands out for its shrill colouring, on its pole on the facade of the building. This place is the nerve centre of the composition, the mid point between interior and exterior. In crossing it, Picasso plunges us towards

the urban landscape in which the statue of Christopher Columbus, one of Barcelona's most representative monuments, stands before the sea.

Once again Picasso shows us his obsession with space and its depth. He delights us with a sagely executed oil in which he blends the faceting of planes in the interior, more open than preceding years, with a more naturalistic, expressionistic style for the exterior, in which in some places the brushwork displays the divisionism similar to what he used in 1901 in *Margot* and *The Dwarf.*

Gored Horse

Unsigned and undated (Barcelona, 1917)
Charcoal on canvas
80.2 x 103.3 cm
Donated by the artist, 1970
MPB 110.012

From his childhood on Picasso had a lifelong passion for bullfighting and during his stay in Barcelona he was again a frequent visitor to the bullring. In a letter dated 18 October 1917 to his friend Apollinaire in Paris, he says: "I bumped into Picabia on Sunday at the bullfight".

So it is no surprise to find the bullfighting theme reappearing in his work. To some extent it links up with another major subject of the time, the world of dance, since both, albeit in different ways, are choreographical.

Here the horse is the focus of the artist's attention. The disembowelled horse, dying with a moving gesture of pain which departs from the picturesque, colourist representation of Manet to approach the horses bleeding to death of Goya and Solana, and of Picasso himself in some works of 1901.

Gored Horse is the synthesis of a series of drawings of this period. Alone in the face of death, the animal collapses and falls on its knees in a fetal or praying position. In appearance it has even been likened to a crustacean or fossilised bird. The pain is so sharp that it stretches its neck and raises its head, staring at the sky, as if begging for mercy to finally end its cruel agony. The concave mouth is a formula of pathos that we have already observed in some Picasso figures of the blue period. The artist thus gives the wretched creature a twofold condition, both animal and human. But the drama of the work reaches its high point in the horn that emerges from the earth, threatening the horse, waiting to kill it when it finally collapses.

With a firm, vigorous line done with charcoal on a sepia canvas, Picasso models the figure of the animal with an exquisite formal quality and marked expressionism. In spite of the distance in time, it is clearly a precedent to *Guernica*.

GLASS AND PACKET OF TOBACCO

Unsigned. Dated *1924* on frame
Oil on canvas
16 x 22 cm; with frame, 36 x 42 cm
Sabartés Collection
MPB 70.243

One of the few works from the inter-war period (1917-1940) in the Museum is this *Glass and Packet of Tobacco*, of 1924. In the course of that year and the following one, Picasso returned to experimenting forcefully with the still life genre, one of the most important in his artistic career.

Picasso's still lifes of this period display a marked shift towards abstraction. At the same time they linked up with the newly created surrealist canons which vigorously proclaimed the need for renewal in aesthetic manifestations, which dreams and the unconsious were held to be of essential value.

This small oil bears witness once again to Picasso's conception of everyday objects as a vehicle for his thought. He once artist told his companion Françoise Gilot: "(...) the objects that enter my painting (...) are ordinary: a jug, a glass of beer, a pipe, a packet of tobacco." They are as ordinary as the ones used by Cézanne. And Cézanne contributed to Picasso's development as a still life painter, although the contributions to the genre made by Rousseau and, much earlier, Zurbarán and Chardin, were decisive.

The description of the objects that make up this composition is highly synthetic, very brief. Picasso did this with voluble, undulating lines, narrower in some places and thicker in others. The simplification of the elements puts the oil one step away from abstraction. He gives the objects and their immediate space an exceptional brightness, resolved with a harmonious combination of ochres and blues which stand out from the dark background. But Picasso's subtlety also makes itself felt in the frame, which he painted with soft, delicate tones, which beyond giving the composition a feeling of unity and balance, makes it more complete.

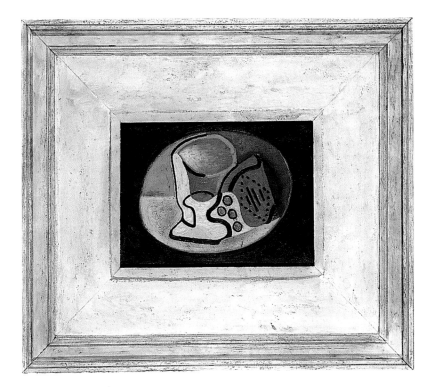

89

PORTRAIT OF JAUME SABARTÉS WITH RUFF AND HAT

Signed *Picasso*. Dated *Royan/22.10.39* lower right.
Oil on canvas
46 x 38 cm
Sabartés Collection
MPB 70.241

Picasso was in the habit of characterising his friends in the most im-plausible ways. So it is not odd that his intimate friend and private secretary should be one of those most often at the receiving end of his extraordinary sense of humour..

In fact Sabartés himself urged Picasso to carry out such a praise-worthy undertaking. On one occasion the two men were locked in a theoretical argument about the portrait. Sabartés told him he wan-ted to be portrayed "with a ruff, like the gentlemen of the 16th cen-tury, and with a plumed hat to cover my head." A few days after this conversation, in December 1938, Picasso dedicated three drawings to Sabartés, which are in the Museum: in one, he wears a monk's ha-bit; in the other two he wears a ruff, one in a hat and one without. The culmination of the series of whimsical portraits requested by Sa-bartés is this oil, which Picasso painted in the October of the follow-ing year in Royan.

Here he subjected the figure of his friend to dislocations which completely break the axis of the head and make it totally ambi-guous. By means of soft, flowing, counterposed lines, he shapes the face which, despite the dislocation of the facial elements, keeps Sa-bartés's own personality.

The fixed gaze is concealed behind the thick spectacles resting on his cheek instead of his nose; the sharp line of the nose, slightly tur-ned up, which fully shows his left profile, is thrown into greater re-lief.

In this work of subtle colours, seen in the flesh and the top of the hat, ambiguity emerges once again because in spite of the marked de-formations, its disconcerting, almost anguished realism is obvious.

In his book *Picasso, retratos y recuerdos* (Picasso, Portraits and Memories), Sabartés gives a careful description: "... My portrait has all the features of my physiognomy; but only the most essential ones and if Picasso has put them together differently to the way most people see them, he took them from memory, thinking about me, with the intention of rendering them in a painting and organising them in tune with his own sensibility and with the need to construct a har-monious work (...)".

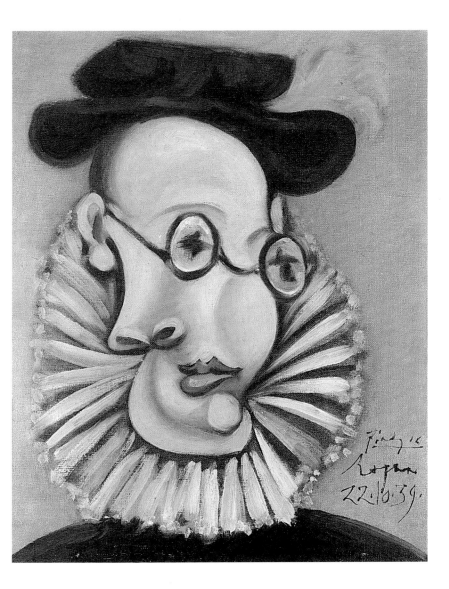

Las Meninas 1957

■

1947	15 May	Birth of Claude, to Françoise Gilot.
	June	Settles in Golfe-Juan with Françoise and Claude.
	August	Starts work as ceramist in Vallauris (Provence)
1948	25 August	Attends Congress of Intellectuals for Peace in Wroclaw, Poland.
	September	Picasso and Françoise move into the Villa La Galloise in Vallauris.
1949	19 April	Birth of daughter Paloma.
	Spring	Buys Fournas studio
1950		Attends World Peace Congress in London.
1953	Summer	Vallauris
	Mid-August	Brief stay in Perpignan (Roussillon) with daughter Maya. Meets Jacqueline Roque.
	Autumn	Separates from Françoise
1954	June	Jacqueline Roque (1927-1986) appears in his painting.
	3 November	Death of Matisse
1955	11 February	Death of Olga Kokhlova
	Summer	Buys La Californie in Cannes and moves in with Jacqueline.
1957	August-December	Paints *Las Meninas*.

LAS MENINAS (GROUP)

■
Unsigned. Dated *17.8.57* on back (Cannes)
Oil on canvas
194 x 260 cm
Donated by the artist, 1968
MPB 70.433

Picasso was not afraid of measuring himself against the great masters of Western painting. On the contrary, he seemed to have a vital need to confront them. So he gave himself over to an exercise through which he analysed and interpreted, with unrivalled voracity, works by artists the likes of Grünewald, Courbet, Manet, El Greco, Velázquez...

The reasons that prompted this laboratory work are many and varied and are perhaps explained by the desire to assure himself that his work could compete with that of his predecessors and to show that the painting of other artists is also an incentive for painting.

In 1952 Picasso and Sabartés got into one of their usual arguments. Picasso said something quite prophetic: "If anyone someone set out to copy *Las Meninas*, in all good faith, let's say, when getting to a certain point, and if the person doing the copying were me, I would say to myself: how would it be if I put this one a little to the right or the left? I would try to do it in my way, forgetting Velázquez. The attempt would lead me, certainly, to modify the light or change it, because of having moved a figure around. So, little by little, I would paint my *Meninas* which would appear detestable to the professional copyist; they wouldn't be the ones he would believe he had seen in Velázquez's canvas, but they would be "my" *Meninas*..."

The variations on a masterpiece of the past led Picasso to systematise the group of canvases with a common theme. Each one is only a part of the whole. The artist says: "it's the movement of the painting, the dramatic effort from one vision to another, even if the effort is not taken to its conclusion (...). I have reached a moment in which the movement of my thought interests me more than my thought itself."

Between August and September 1957, Picasso closed the doors of his studio and began to face the challenge of *Las Meninas* of Velázquez. One work, a unique piece, is the origin of 58 oils —44 inspired by the model, 9 pigeons, 3 landscapes and 2 free interpretations. An entire series! It is an exhaustive study of form, rhythm, colour and movement. A game of the boundless imagination which metamorphoses the figures without varying the original preceptive space, volume and light at all.

The representation begins with a great ensemble which respects the compositional structure of the model while changing the vertical format for the horizontal. Another substantial variation is the opening of the great windows which Velázquez painted shut. It is very well known that Picasso loved light over and above all things. Once he told Apollinaire: "Colours are only symbols and reality exists only in the light." It is a personal vision that sums up Picasso's styles from Cubism on.

Las Meninas is a grand interior scene, the portrait of the studio, probably a spacious room with large windows in the Alcázar of Madrid where Velázquez worked. Suddenly, time stands still in an instant of flashing life and freezes the image. With sublime perfection Picasso, like Velázquez, captures the air of the surroundings and the naturalness of the scene going on in the spacious palace room.

The figures do not vary. Picasso even keeps the two principal trios: Velázquez, Agustina de Sarmiento and the Infanta Margarita, and Isabel de Velasco, Maribárbola and Nicolasito and also Eco, the sitting dog. What changes is the aesthetic representation. It starts, on the left, with a tightly closed artistic language —Velázquez, whom he enlarges considerably and in whose hands he puts two palettes for work on the canvas, also enlarged— and, as he moves to the right, the figures and elements that form the composition lose substance and the form is more simplified and elliptic -Nicolasito Pertusato. There is no colour. The chromatic richness of Velázquez disappears and the work turns into grisaille, like the black and white photo Picasso kept at home.

LAS MENINAS (MARÍA AGUSTINA SARMIENTO)

Unsigned. Dated *20./8./57* and *57* (erased), and *26* on back (Cannes)
Oil on canvas
46 x 37.5 cm
Donated by the artist, 1968
MPB 70.435

Posssessed by an avid desire for research, Picasso carried out a true laboratory job which pushed him to explore a reality of his own. "Inquiring, unceasing, perservering and tenacious" as Sabartés defines him, he endeavoured to show what is human in each figure.

He straightaway chose María Agustina de Sarmiento, the *dama menina*, the daughter of Diego Sarmiento de Sotomayor and Juana de Iasi Ladrón de Guevara, who became countess of Aguilar and countess of Barajas thanks to her two marriages.

The *meninas* were the young noblewomen who waited on the infanta. Protocol laid down that they should courtsey when serving food to their superior. Picasso painted this moment when, as was the custom, María Agustina, bowing slightly, shows her respect while offering the illustrious girl an earthenware pitcher on a silver tray. It is perhaps in this insignificant everyday act —which the artist had copied from the original in a drawing he made in Madrid in 1897— and which Picasso breaks down in the context of the series, where the most obvious action of the entire scene lies.

Picasso centres all the figure's expressiveness in the overgrown and distorted face of the girl and her out-of-proportion hands. Col-

our returns, timidly, after the great grisaille of the ensemble. Grey does not disappear. On the contrary, it is kept and continues to dominate the composition, though accompanied by a soft blue which sweetens the work. A touch of acid yellow gives brightness to the pitcher on the tray. The flesh, brilliant, is delicately reddened with brushstrokes in pink and earthy tones, very watered down, which contrast with the areas of more pastose brushwork.

Las Meninas (Infanta Margarita María)

Unsigned. Dated 6./9./57 on back (Cannes)
Oil on canvas
46 x 37.5 cm
Donated by the artist, 1968
MPB 70.449

The axis of the composition of *Las Meninas* is the Infanta Margarita María, the daughter of Philip IV and his second wife Mariana of Austria. The infanta was born on 12 July 1651. Bearing in mind this date and Sánchez Cantón's statement that Velázquez painted this exceptional oil at the end of the summer of 1656, we know that the child was then five years old.

Alone —full length or bust— and accompanied by the *meninas*, the *infanta* was the principal focus of Picasso's attention: he devoted fourteen studies exclusively to her.

The bust of the princess takes up the entire canvas. Picasso gave her a more naturalistic treatment. Behind her is just a black background, further highlighting the figure which is treated with a palette reduced to greys, emerald green and light pink brushstrokes for the flesh. Unlike Velázquez, Picasso painted a portrait of princess with a white face, brimming with light, and golden hair.

The close-up of the child, one day to be empress, shows a sharp wide-awake look. The face is clean. The dark, almond-shaped eyes are sheltered beneath arched eyebrows which the artist uses together with the line of the nose to make a spiral play that energises the

face. The snub nose and small, dainty mouth accentuate the girl's fragility. She is shown with well-styled long hair adorned with a posy of flowers which leaves her face uncovered, showing rounded features and chubby cheeks, slightly pink. Picasso's treatment of the girl's face and and square neckline of her dress are similar to Matisse's 1907 *Portrait of Marguerite*, which belonged to his private collection. The brushwork is nervous, loose and bold, highly diluted in some areas, thicker in others.

THE PIGEONS

Unsigned. Dated 6./9./57 on back (Cannes)
Oil on canvas
100 x 80 cm
Donated by the artist, 1968
MPB 70.450

In June 1955, determined to return to the Mediterranean, Picasso bought La Californie in the upper part of Cannes. Built in 1880, the villa was sumptuous and baroque in style, very spacious and surrounded with leafy gardens. This is where *Las Meninas* was born.

When he set himself to interpreting Velázquez's work, which Luca Giordano had defined as "the theology of painting", Picasso cut himself off from his surroundings and locked himself away on the top floor of the villa for four months. Suddenly he interrupted his work of interpretation and became immersed in a series of nine oils on the subject of pigeons.

The new studio had a great veranda over the garden. Beside this was a pigeon house which Picasso himself had had built a year before. It was filled with pigeons of all shapes and colours flying in and out at will.

Picasso had been accompanied by pigeons since childhood, when guided by the hand of his father, José Ruiz Blasco, also a keen painter of these birds, he made his first drawings, which are in the Museum. Now, in the midst of his work of interpretation, he took a brief respite to meet again with his old friends.

While some pigeons rest in the house, others peck at food on the ground and a third group perches on the railing —one has already flown off— and watch the bay of Cannes with the Leirin Islands in the background. All the spaces in the painting are compartmentalised with a thick black outline and painted with bright colours that give the work a structure in relief. The veranda is wide open and lets in all the Mediterranean light producing an exuberant explosion of colour. The pigeons, the vegetation, the sea... the elements of everyday reality shine with dazzling colour.

THE PIGEONS

Unsigned. Dated *12.9./57* and *14.9./57* on back (Cannes)
Oil on canvas
100 x 80 cm
Donated by the artist, 1968
MPB 70.456

The result of Picasso's self-imposed isolation to tackle *Las Meninas* —described by Sabartés in the words of Góngora: "To my solitude I go, from my solitude I come, because to get along with myself, my thoughts suffice"— was nine paintings: eight large format and one small one, with pigeons as their main subject. These works, along with three small landscapes which also form part of the series, enabled Picasso to establish a stimulating conceptual play mixing external reality and pictorial reality, or what amounts to the same: life and art.

A vital need for freedom impelled him to show us these birds which had lived in his work since his childhood.

In the nine oils of the pigeon house and its inhabitants, Picasso shows us part of the interior and immediately turns us towards the outside. We thus reencounter a traditional theme in his work: the window, a functional motif, an element of communication between the two perspective spaces. This theme was also handled well by Matisse, whom Picasso greatly admired. The scene starts from inside the house, where several coloured chicks rest in nests, while the others, white, peck at food on the ground. Then, after the veranda with railings outlined in black and white, Picasso plunges us towards the leafy

vegetation of the garden, filled with trees rising against the blue of the Mediterranean which is radiant with light. Picasso spares no detail in the description, a touch baroque. The interior spaces are well structured with brightly coloured contour lines. The palette is bold and vibrant, the brushwork loose and nervous. The whole work is dazzlingly resplendent.

Las Meninas (Infanta Margarita María)

Unsigned. Dated *14./9./57* on back (Cannes)
Oil on canvas
100 x 81 cm
Donated by the artist, 1968
MPB 70.459

To judge from the portraits painted by Velázquez, the Infanta Margarita María appears to have been a lively, pleasant girl, not pretty but charming and elegant.

Picasso painted the infanta in the typical clothing of the nobility of the period. The neck of the embroidered lamé gown has a trimming of flowers, a typical decorative motif of the 17th century which Picasso turns into a pure patch of colour.

In the figure, the forms are given a simplified, geometric treatment. The space is constructed through juxtaposed planes with exuberant colouring, accentuated by the dark treatment of the background. The face, too large in proportion to the body, has a very suggestive pictorial writing because of the geometric fragmentation, allowing it to be crossed with strips of green, black, blue and white.

From the luxuriant workmanship of Velázquez Picasso kept the vigorous interpretation of the flesh, the silk and the subtle light of the clothing which, in this oil, translates into white lines and daubs

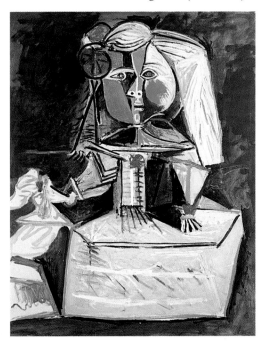

over the bright green gown and its blue contour.

The girl holds out her right arm and takes the pitcher on the silver tray that is held by a *menina* who did not fit into the pictorial space. The infanta's left hand has schematic features, done with primitive drawing, typical of Picasso's late style.

Las Meninas (group without Velázquez)

Unsigned. Dated *15./9./57* on back (Cannes)
Oil on canvas
129 x 161 cm
Donated by the artist, 1968
MPB 70.460

It was said that at the Alcázar, as well as Philip IV, boredom reigned. Lope de Vega was wont to say that "at the Palace, even the figures in the tapestries yawn." Only one room escaped the daily torpor: Velázquez's studio. Palomino explained that both Philip IV and his wife Mariana and the "infantas and ladies" used to go and watch him paint "which they loved as a pleasant delight and entertainment."

Picasso turned again to the horizontal format he used in the great initial grisaille to produce a series of large-format compositions. In this oil, the first in the series, he systematised a new artistic language.

Picasso cut out and froze the central part of the painting. The sensation of paralysed movement is stronger than ever. The attitudes and gazes of the figures in the centre, the infanta and the two *meninas*, give off a challenging expressive power. Picasso treats these ladies,

as he does most of the other figures that form the composition, with a careful sense of caricature. The geometric cutting of the flat forms, brightly coloured and highlighted with simplified features and with a unified green-blue ground, still show through the compartmenta-lisation inherited from the stained glass window and the etching. The brushwork is smooth and diluted. The predominance of green-blue, which spreads throughout the compositional space, gives the work a mysterious and at the same time melancholy air.

But much of the attention of this paraphrase falls on the mirror, an illusionist element that Velázquez used to make the presence of the monarchs real; in this oil it becomes a focus for the projection of the space, the real protagonist of the masterpice, which above all is a *cosa mentale*, as Leonardo da Vinci wanted his works to be.

LAS MENINAS (GROUP)

Unsigned. Dated *15./9./57* on back (Cannes)
Oil on canvas
161 x 129 cm
Donated by the artist, 1968
MPB 70.464

Repetition as a medium of creation is one of the symptomatic elements of Picasso's late periods. Then, he favoured the series, the set, variations in respect of the concept of the single masterpiece. With repetition, he was interested above all in the mechanism of creation, in the process, in the quest for perfection. He once said: "If I search for truth in my canvas, I can make a hundred canvases with this truth."

Seized with a great creative desire, the urge to analyse, to decompose and recompose Velázquez's masterpiece with no limits, led

him to undertake, within the series itself, a small repertoire of large-format compositions which seem to be correlative on account of the rhythms and counterhythms developed in them, and, also because of the stylistic treatment, which shifts from austere geometric forms to a tense rococo.

Once again Picasso used the device of the flat painting and structures the work by means of planes of colour, predominantly reds and blacks. The figures present a simple, naked workmanship achieved with screens of vivid colour. For the upper limbs, he repeated the primitive drawing we have seen in other oils in the series. He had a vital need to schematise. The figures that most felt the consequences are those of Marcela Ulloa, who was second head lady-in-waiting from 1643, and the chief of the ladies-in-waiting Diego Ruiz de Azcona Escaleras, who have almost turned into furniture. Their faces are asterisks and their hands, simplified to the maximum, are disproportionately large. The painter Diego da Silva Velázquez has disappeared, his own work concealing him. He keeps the "chamberlain" in the open doorway which leads into another space. Here we should recall Picasso's fascination for open doors, windows and mirrors which he used to tackle perspective. Sometimes, as here, the opening is preceeded by the shadow of a human figure, sometimes not.

Las Meninas (group)

Unsigned. Dated *2./10./57* on back (Cannes)
Oil on canvas
161 x 129 cm
Donated by the artist, 1968
MPB 70.465

Throughout the interpretative discourse of *Las Meninas*, Picasso always maintained the dual attitude of the master of the Spanish Golden Age, Velázquez, who presented at one and the same time the surprise of the unexpected visit and the intellectual enigma.

Exorcised by the banal scene, which is seductive for an artist, like Velázquez he offers us the moment when the infanta-girl bursts headlong into Velazquez's studio while he contemplates the great canvas on the easel.

Velázquez returns to a normal size, while the canvas is still enlarged. Oddly, if we observe all the *Las Meninas* series, we see that the figure of Velázquez only appears in four works.

In the initial composition, as mentioned above, Picasso keeps the two principal trios in the central part, the dog in the foreground and the background figures. He does so in this oil, too. All look at the spectators, situated in front of the painting, where plausibly the king and queen are, reflected in the mirror.

The baroque treatment of the forms reaches its maximum. Picasso's painting turns into a veritable orgy of forms and colours, elab-

orated with a closed artistic language which crosses the painting diagonally from left to right. In the centre, the infanta acts as a link. Surprisingly, at the top of the canvas and in the lower right margin, the forms are more simplified and the planes of bright colours more generous and well defined, so that they make the hermetic writing of the rest of the composition disappear. In all it constitutes, as Leymarie would say, a good "little castle of rectangles".

Unsigned. Dated *10.10/57/III* on back (Cannes)
Oil on canvas
115 x 89 cm
Donated by the artist, 1968
MPB 70.471

Picasso focused on Agustina Sarmiento in five oils. In this one he presents a full-length portrait of her. His detailed reading offers us a strong-minded and obliging girl, elaborated with an extraordinary analytical and creative capacity. The totally subjective interpretation keeps the slight bow of respect when serving food to the infanta. The face of the girl shows the proliferation of geometric forms. The hands are expressive and large, out of proportion, and accentuate the action.

The predominance of green, filled wth nuances, gives the work great plastic beauty. Picasso spares no details in the description of the clothing of the girl, who is vain like her mistress. The clothes, well cut and of quality texture, shimmer reflecting the light. The girl's reddish hair is gathered up with a square green and white slide. Everything accentuates the graceful charm of the young lady of the court.

The *menina* was the lady-in-waiting to the infanta. In fact, this was a Portuguese word also used for pageboys. Originally, Velázquez's

painting was called *La Familia*. In the Museo del Prado catalogue drawn up by Pedro de Madrazo in 1843, the painting was first mentioned with the title *Las Meninas*, in Portuguese "the girls". It is a relatively modern name, from the Romantic period, which has come down to our own days.

THE PIANO

Unsigned and undated. (Cannes, 17 October, 1957)
Oil on canvas
130 x 96 cm
Donated by the artist, 1968
MPB 70.472

The person dealt with by Picasso in *The Piano*, with an extraodinary sense of humour and some irony, is Nicolas de Portosanto or Pertusato, the Italian dwarf who entertained the young ladies at the court of the Austrias. He was so well proportioned that rather than a dwarf he looked like a child. Velázquez had painted him with his hands in the air and his left foot on the snoozing dog. This posture precisely suggests to Picasso the presence of the musical instrument: "I have seen a dwarf with a piano (...) The piano came into my head and I couldn't help but put it somewhere (...) This happens many times when I am painting, and these images form part of the reality of the subject (...)".

Picasso presents the chubby buffoon in an ingenious and creative way, at a keyboard, in the light of two candles, with outlandish clothes in garish red. His body moves in time to the music which his hands cause to issue from the great harmonic piece of furniture. His head is a round white patch which slides towards his back through a long plait.

The charm of the scene lies in the sincere, fresh capturing of the instant. "The role of painting is to freeze movement" as Picasso once said.

In front, Velázquez's aristo dog is replaced by Lump, the basset hound then incumbent at La Californie, who displays the Picassian distorsions throughout the series.

107

Las Meninas (Isabel de Velasco and María Bárbola)

Unsigned. Dated *8.11./57.* on back (Cannes)
Oil on canvas
130 x 96 cm
Donated by the artist, 1968
MPB 70.477

In this sequence, Picasso presents the full image of the *menina* Isabel de Velasco, the daughter of the count and countess of Colmenares, and the macrocephalous handmaiden of German extraction María Bárbola. Once again their spontaneity astonishes us. The diary written zealously by Picasso, permanently captivated by Velázquez, again disturbs us with the creative capacity and plastic beauty of this work painted in early November.

Picasso centred the composition on the two figures, although the picture gets its drama from Maribárbola, who assumes an almost defiant attitude. Her hands, like claws, and upper limbs, are highly graphic and done in a primitive, immediate style. They seem to want to stop us in our tracks. Picasso covered her face with a transparent veil which filters the image of an almost monstrous and extremely aggressive face. Meanwhile, the round-faced *menina* looks at her out of the corner of her eye. Picasso displayed great ingenuity in his resolving the textures of the transparent veils of the girls and extraordinary graphic purity in the gowns, which are structured in well-outlined planes in cold colours contrasting with the warmth of the red background and the brilliant yellow of the floor. As in the other works in the series, Picasso gave himself over to a portentous exercise in style.

PORTRAIT OF JACQUELINE

Unsigned. Dated *3.12.57* on right (Cannes)
Oil on canvas
116 x 89 cm
Donated by the artist, 1968
MPB 70.489

In the summer of 1954 Picasso met Jacqueline Roque, with whom he shared the last twenty years of life. She was a constant presence in his final struggle against time, when he took the painting as a model. At that time Picasso said: "I have less and less time and more and more to say."

This work is one of the two free interpretations —the other is *The Piano*— with which he recreated the *Las Meninas* suite, based on the masterpiece of the man who once made him exclaim subtly "Velázquez!"

From the outset Jacqueline was privy to the secret, so well kept until the end. Only she and Sabartés had the privilege of following the battle between the two masters, who alongside Goya, are "the alpha and omega" of Spanish painting.

This is the image of a sober, reserved, modest Jacqueline, which is how those who know her define her. She is dressed austerely, in black. Only one note of colour adorns her: the emerald green ribbon from forehead to nape of neck, where she is naked beneath her hair tied back in a tail. The ribbon highlights the classical profile of

the face, with almond-shaped eyes, arched eyebrows and straight nose. She sits in a blue-black chair which stands out energetically from the red background and collides on the right with the bright yellow frame. The work once again evokes the studio of Velázquez and its walls filled with works of art, the vision of which suggested to Picasso the introduction in the series of painting, the painting of the painting. In this way, perhaps, he wishes to indicate that *Las Meninas* are both variations and the apotheosis of the interior of a studio.

In effect, *Las Meninas* are the studio par excellence.

The Last Years 1958-1973

1958	*September*	Picasso buys Vauvernages Castle (Aix-en-Provence)
1960		The Picasso Museum of Barcelona is founded with the donation of the Jaume Sabartés collection, with the addition of Picasso's works in the collection of the Museu d'Art Modern.
1961	*2 March*	Marriage of Picasso and Jacqueline Roque in Vallauris.
	June	They move into the Mas Notre-Dame-de-Vie, in Mougins.
1962		Intense activity as printmaker, for the next ten years.
1963	*9 March*	Opening of the Picasso Museum of Barcelona.
1968	*13 February*	Death of Sabartés. Picasso pays tribute to him by donating the *Las Meninas* suite and other works to the Museum.
1970	*January*	Major donation by Picasso to the Museum of the works kept at his family's home in Barcelona.
	1 May-30 September	*Pablo Picasso 1969-1970* exhibition at the Popes' Palace at Avignon.
1973	*8 April*	Death of Picasso at Notre-Dame-de-Vie, in Mougins.
	10 April	Picasso buried in the garden of his castle at Vauvernages.
	23 May-23 September	*Pablo Picasso 1970-1972* exhibition at the Popes' Palace at Avignon.

Signed *Picasso* bottom left and dated *31.3.65 II* on back of canvas.
Oil on canvas
100 x 81 cm
Bought in March 1968
MPB 70.810

A look at Picasso's oeuvre reveals its gradual mutation. The new freedoms succeed each other but do not cause a rupture. Between 1963 and 1965 he appears to have gone mad in a frenzied desire to paint. On the back cover of a 1963 album of drawings he wrote: "Painting is stronger than me; it does what it wants with me." Canvases emerge one after the other. Their common denominator is to materialise art in its practice. Then, the theme of the painter and model and all its variants re-emerged powerfully. The confrontation between the two: the model alone, the place of creation —the studio— ... and the painter alone, as in this oil. We see the artist bearded, alone, working on his canvas. His glance is restless and penetrating. The right eye is shaped like crochet hook, a graphic element which is repeated insistently in Picasso's late work.

The theme of painter and model had already made its appearance in his youthful work and emerged in filigree throughout his life, to the point of being regarded as a pictorial subgenre within his oeuvre. However it was during the last twenty years of his life (1953-1973) that it reached its peak and the painting became model, subject or example.

In *Painter at Work*, some formal aspects of his late style, from 1964, begin to make their presence felt. He invented a new pictorial script founded on an absolute freedom and spontaneity. Particularly salient features are the shorthand style, the materiality of the painting, the brushwork at times very thick, at times flowing, the marked brush lines... in short, an aesthetic that is primitive, brutal and sometimes *non finito*.

In his old age Picasso returned to childhood, to naivety and freshness of vision. As has been said, after learning all there was to learn, he left it all, the result being a great sincerity of gesture and infinite freedom of treatment of the pictorial space. This is clear in this painting of subtle pinks, blues and greys, pale and tender, complemented with gleaming white to make a picture brimming with light.

113

Seated Man

Signed and dated *24.6.69/ Picasso* top right.
Oil on cardboard
129 x 65 cm
MPB 112.867

In his last years Picasso takes us by surprise with an aesthetic and formal revolution poorly understood at the time. After shaking up the Renaissance legacy with an attack on one of its foundations, illusionist perspective, with cubism, he again threw out a challenge creating a new pictorial space and opening up new avenues in the plastic arts.

In the notion of the late work we find the final renovation of a pictorial script able to awaken the most diverse feelings. Picasso freed himself from all knowledge, all technique and returned to what is natural, to spontaneity, to the infancy of art, to primitive, immediate and wild painting... In a word, to painting without rules or restraints, an expression of his prodigious energy, which gave him life until his last moments.

Seated Man is a clear exponent of this painting of transgression of what is known as the Avignon period, in virtue of the two major exhibitions staged at the Papal Palace (1970 and 1973). There Picasso offered a series of archetypes, one being the hybrid monster of this oil, in which the human and the coarsest animalness merge. From the mixture emerges this intriguing character described primitively and vehemently with contrasts of well comparmentalised colours with black outlines, thick and crude.

To elaborate the ambiguous face, Picasso returned to the mask, as symbol and fetish. It is one of the tarot cards of Avignon which in the end he used to carry out his research, as previously he made use of African and Oceanian masks or Romanesque art. The facial features are animal while the hair and colossal moustache and goatee are direct referents of the grand gentlemen of the Spanish Golden Age.

The ascent of the monster clearly reflects his need to show convulsive beauty. It shows the desire to express an obsessive, fantastic universe through a primary, brutal aesthetic. Again undertaking the *non finito*, he displays the materiality of paintings, with overloaded tones, crude lines, smeared areas, and graphic elements characteristic of this last period such as the hands in the form of a fan he always shows face on.

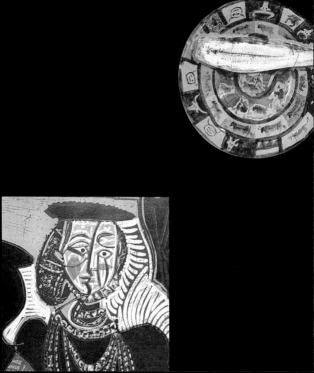

The Prints

■

The Picasso Museum of Barcelona has an important collection of prints and lithographs by Picasso, comprising some 1500 items.

Some were donated by his friend and personal secretary, Jaume Sabartés, one of the authors of the museum. A large part of the collection was donated by Picasso himself when he paid tribute to Sabartés on his death and undertook to give, for the rest of his life, a copy of every print created by him. The rest are donations from other benefactors and purchases made by the Museum.

The works in this collection are also a living testimony to Picasso's close relationship with important printers such as Eugène Delâtre, Louis Fort, Roger Lacourière, Aldo and Piero Crommelynck, Mourlot and Arnéra, with each of whom he established a profitable working relationship. The dialogue between printmaker and printer resulted in one of the most important legacies of prints in the history of the graphic arts.

We never tire of repeating that Picasso has undoubtedly been the greatest printmaker this century, not only in terms of quantity —more than 2,000 works— and quality, but also because of the creative and technical innovations he brought to the genre.

Picasso's first incursion into this field was in 1899 when he etched a picador on a plate. Whether through inexperience or deliberately we do not know, the man holding the pike is left-handed, hence the title: *El zurdo* (The Left-handed One). In printmaking, the printed image is the reverse of that of the plate, so we will never be sure whether *El zurdo* was really left-handed or this was just a mistake made by the novice printmaker. The important thing is that Picasso's constancy and creative genius led him, year after year, to consolidate the craft until he became one of the great printmakers in the history of art: a pinnacle shared only with the great masters of printmaking of all time: Dürer, Rembrandt, Piranesi and Goya.

The Museum's collection of prints starts with *The Frugal Repast* (1904), which was to mark the true beginning of his

117

activity in this field. It is an etching made by Picasso in Paris with the Catalan painter and printmaker Ricard Canals. Thematically and aesthetically it belongs fully to the blue period. The two languishing figures with their blank gaze lean on a table. They are the diners at a meal devoid of food. The Museum has proof number 2, which Picasso kept. Delâtre made a first, brief run. Then, in 1913, Vollard commissioned another from the printer Fort.

From then until his death, Picasso explored the different techniques of printmaking: woodcut, etching, aquatint, drypoint, lithography, silk-screen printing...

From the cubist period there are four etchings made in Cadaqués, in 1911, to illustrate the text of the poet Max Jacob *Saint Matorel*, of 1910. These were published by his dealer D.H. Kahnweiler and printed by Delâtre.

In the twenties, the subjects and aesthetics of Picasso's prints ran parallel to those of his painting. In this collection there is a set of drypoints and etchings on a variety of subjects: mother and child, portraits of Olga, still lifes, bathers, heads of men and women...

In 1931, the Swiss publisher Albert Skira brought out

The Frugal Repast Ovid's *Metamorphoses* with the printer Louis Fort, illustra-

ted with 30 etchings on mythological subjects. The copy here in the was donated by Salvador Dalí in 1963.

Another outstanding series was published by Picasso's dealer Ambroise Vollard in 1939. Known as the *Suite Vollard*, this is a set of 100 works, basically etchings, drypoints and aquatints. The Museum has thirty of these, made by Picasso between 1930 and 1937, which were compiled by the publisher. The *Suite Vollard* comprises 27 plates with no specific subjects and 73 which fall into five thematic groups: "The Rape" (5),

Minotauromaquia "The Sculptor's Studio" (46), "Rembrandt" (4), "Minotaur" and "Blind Minotaur" (15) and 3 portraits of Vollard himself. As he did in the other plastic fields, Picasso introduced a new model into printmaking, Marie-Thérèse Walter (1909-1977), who shared several years of his life and the mother of his daughter Maya. This pleasant, round-faced woman inspired the handsome set of sculptures of Boisgeloup and prompted him to take the theme of sculptor and model to printmaking, whereby she became the model par excellence of those years.

The "Minotaur" plays a major role in the Suite Vollard and in one of Picasso's supreme prints, *La Minotauromàquia*, one of the best of the 20th century. This is an etching with scratching, of perfect workmanship, done in the spring of 1935 and printed by Lacourière. It is regarded as one of the immediate precedents of the *Guernica* (1937).

It is well known that throughout the Spanish Civil War (1936-1939), Picasso always stood up for Republican Spain. In order to raise funds, on 8 January 1937 he printed the two etchings entitled *Sueño* (Dream) and *Mentira de Franco* (Franco's Lie). In a series of vignettes, he recounted the deeds of an evil character of monstrous appearance. He is followed

119

Portrait of a Lady after Cranach the Younger

by a series of weeping women, like the one in one of the compartments of one of the etchings, who reveal their great grief at the magnitude of the tragedy.

After World War II (1939-1945), Picasso's print-making was dominated for some time by lithography. This collection shows the variety of subjects he tackled during these years: the woman —now his partner Françoise Gilot— the woman-flower, the still life, the bull... and a series of interpretations of works of the past such as David and Bathsheba according to Cranach. But the most emblematic figure of these years of pacification is the pigeon, which became the centre of some of these lithographs. We should recall that the poet Aragon chose one for the poster for the first Peace Congress, held in Paris in 1949.

At that time, Picasso also became highly active as a book illustrator, and the Museum has a good selection of these: *Deux contes* (1947) by Ramon Reventós; *Vingt poèmes* (1948) by Luís de Góngora y Argote; *À haute flamme* (1955) by Tristan Tzara; *Dans l'atelier de Picasso* (1957) and *Les Menines et la vie* (1958) by Jaume Sabartés; *Sable mouvant* (1966) by Pierre Reverdy; *El entierro del Conde Orgaz* (1969) by Pablo Picasso. Of this last-named title, as well as the prints, the Museum owns the annulled copper plates and a copy made from these.

During the decade from 1954 to 1964, Picasso devoted himself intensively to the linocut. At Vallauris he met the printer Arnéra with whom he established a fruitful exchange leading led to the production of 200 linocuts of which the Museum has around 70. The technical innovations Picasso brought to this medium consolidated their identity and changed the procedure, making it faster and better quality. In *Portrait of a Lady after Cranach the Younger*, of 1958, Picasso was still using the traditional method of making one plate for each printing. The following summer he completely revolutionised the technique. The whole process was carried out on a single plate which was engraved and cleaned after each printing. With the new method, he made the series of prints that forms part of the interpretative set of Manet's *Le déjeuner sur l'herbe*, and the beautiful portraits of Jacqueline, the woman who shared the last twenty years of his life.

Meanwhile, between 1957 and 1959, he produced a series dedicated to the art of bullfighting. A set of 27 aquatints to illustrate the book *Tauromaquia o Arte de torear* (The Art of Bullfighting) by José Delgado, known as *Pepe Illo*. Picasso presented the whole process of the bullfight, from the preceding moments to the death of a the bull, with an excellent vision of bullfighting comparable only to Goya's. The Museum has the prints made from the annulled plates and also these, but without the corresponding text.

The last years of Picasso's life stand out for two major series of prints. These are the series of the *347* and the *156* prints, which are the thematic and iconographic epilogue to his years as a creator. He made the first between 16 March and 5 October 1968, and gave an entire run to the Museum between December 1968 and September 1971. The second was printed by the Crommelynck brothers, and Picasso's family

Bullfight.
MPB 112.770

La Celestina
MPB 112.028

donated it through the Louise Leiris gallery in 1980 (one item is missing). This donation also included two aquatints: *Venus and Cupid according to Cranach the Younger* (1949) and the *Portrait of Angela Rosengart* (1966). The 155 prints in the series of 156 form a homogeneous set because they were the last ones made by Picasso, between 24 November 1968 and 25 March 1972. They are artist's proofs, the I/XV signed with an inking pad, with the exception of four which were signed and dedicated personally to Jaume Sabartés.

In 1983, respecting Picasso's wishes, his heirs and Louise Leiris gave the city of Barcelona 117 prints representative of the classical period, the surrealist-linked period and the Mediterranean period. It is a handsome group displaying the great variety of techniques used by Picasso: etching, aquatint, drypoint, lithograph and burin.

122

Picasso the Ceramist

■

Following centuries of artistic specialisation, at the end of the 19th century and above all at the beginning of this one, with the fauvists and cubists the complete artist reemerged. Picasso is one of the leading representatives.

New conceptual approaches in the plastic arts compelled artists to employ a variety of means for investigation and execution. Ceramics was one. This technique, the most ancestral of all, became the synthesis of painting and sculpture.

Chance put Picasso on the road to ceramics. Summering at Golfe-Juan in 1946, a friend introduced him to Suzanne and Georges Ramié, proprietors of the Madoura studio in Vallauris, which they invited him to visit. Driven by curiosity, Picasso modelled a few small figures in clay.

The following summer he returned with a number of projects under his arm. This was the start of intense activity that lasted for years. Picasso threw himself into the new task with the same vitality as he put into his drawing, painting, print-making and sculpture. He was sixty-six when he took on the new challenge: the adventure of ceramics.

His insatiable curiosity would not allow him to miss out on the challenges of this technique. Here were new materials with their properties and quirks to discover and new techniques to find for handling them. How could he resist the mystery of the process of creating ceramics? The starting point, the formless mass of clay; the modelling, by hand or on the wheel, of the form from the material; the decoration with muted colours which only reveal their identity on emergence from the kiln... It was all far too fascinating to miss!

Picasso spiritedly tackled the new support, the new materials, the new colours, the test by fire, the firing and its surprises.

In the late forties he alternated between Paris and the French Midi. In 1948 he rented the La Galloise villa, owned by his friend the printer Fort, and in 1949 he bought the big Fournas warehouses where there were three workshops. One he devoted to sculpture, one to painting and one to ceramics. Until 1955 when he moved to La Californie, he produced his ceramics there and fired them at the Madoura workshop.

His work in this field was revolutionary. But traditional ceramists, not without reason, called it the work of a heretic, for Picasso used rather unorthodox resources in all the phases of manufacture: support, decoration and firing. Suzanne and Georges Ramié were wont to say that an apprentice who worked like Picasso would never find employment.

Broadly speaking, there are two main aspects to Picasso's work as a ceramist. In one, ceramics has links with painting; Picasso enhanced plates, platters, vases with colour, as well as highlighting luminosity and experimenting with drawing and colour on non-flat surfaces. In the other, the most important, he created his own forms, often using existing supports which he modified on the wheel or by hand.

As far as supports are concerned, anything would do: from the traditional —plates, elongated or round platters, Spanish plates, Gothic jugs, vases— to the more industrial —pots, two-handled jars, tiles, bricks— to the most unusual — a sort of Roman table used as a support for the pieces fired in the kiln— to the most unheard of —debris from dumps to which he gave a new identity.

Often, he intervened in the earthenware pieces to the point of metamorphosing them surprisingly, the ceramist turning into sculptor. And Picasso, as Kahnweiler says, had for quite some time been seeking the union of painting and sculpture, which he appeared to achieve in his ceramic works.

Nor was decoration easy, for it had to be thought out in line with the form and volume of the support. And the colours, as mentioned above, are deceptive. The effects of the metal oxides which are used to treat the piece cannot be judged beforehand: the ceramist's palette emerges into the light after firing. In addition to all this, Picasso often made empirical or anarchic use of the mediums, from mixing slips, enamels, pastels, glazes, to adding a patina, making incisions, scraping...

But there can be no doubt that despite his heterodoxy, which resulted in more than one fright, his technical boldness and the beauty of his works made him an exceptional ceramist.

The culmination of his career as a ceramist was the invention of printed ceramics, which he used exhaustively between 1949 and 1971. Picasso printed cliches which he printed on a lamina of smoothened paste. With reproduction on clay he surpassed the traditional material for making prints, paper, and opened up new avenues of plastic expression.

With regard to decoration, sometimes he respected the form, sometimes he totally disarranged it. His iconographic repertoire is quite precise, though innovative, because as a general rule he stays away from the great decorative traditions. Some themes were regular ones which he transferred to other plastic fields: bullfighting, Mediterranean mythology and its characters, the still life... Others are fugitives from works such as *Las Meninas*. Still others are from the animal world: sea creatures, mammals, birds...

His palette was varied. Although the pieces were usually fired at low temperatures, which gives them vibrant colouring, a substantial amount of the decoration was done with a cool range: blacks, whites, greys, sepias... Often white was the only colour of the piece.

Picasso's ceramics are handsomely represented in the Museum with forty-two works donated by Jacqueline Picasso in 1982. These comprise round, rectangular and oval plates, pots, vases, most of red or white clay, decorated with slip or metal oxides, manganese and copper oxides. Some display incisions, others reliefs and printed motifs, some are partially glazed.

The Spanish plate *Scene of a Race with Fish* stands out for its decoration and the mixture of materials: manganese oxide on wax reserves and the relief of the fish with varnished slip. In the white series mentioned is the oval plate *White Face*. Picasso used the platters to depict bullfighting scenes, portraying placid animals and bacchanalian scenes with dancers and flute-players, male characters, watchful owls and fish swimming in the depths of the sea. He uses the pots to portray his faithful partner Jacqueline and to represent two of his favourite animals, the pigeon and the goat. He found vases ideal for rings of *sardana* dancers, or their sensual forms for the nude female body. But, like he does in the *Portrait of Jacqueline* from the *Las Meninas* series where the artist makes the painting of the painting, Picasso also makes ceramics of ceramics with the Vases vase. Most of the ceramic pieces bear the stamp *Madoura Plein Feu* on the reverse side and some also have Picasso's *Empreinte Originale* stamp.

Sardana jug
MPB 112.450

Basic Bibliography

Buildings

AINAUD DE LASARTE, Joan: "Els palaus del carrer Montcada" in The Catalogue of Drawing and Painting of the Picasso Museum. Barcelona, Ajuntament de Barcelona, 1984.

AINAUD DE LASARTE, Joan: *Pintures del segle XIII al carrer de Montcada de Barcelona. Barcelona.* Reial Acadèmia de Bones Lletres de Barcelona, 1969.

CIRICI, Alexandre: *Barcelona pam a pam.* Barcelona, Editorial Teide, 4th ed., 1976.

FABRE. J. and HUERTAS CLAVERIA, J.M.: *Tots els barris de Barcelona.* Barcelona, Edicions 62, 1977, contr. 5.

FLORENSA, Adolfo: *La calle Montcada.* Barcelona, Ayuntamiento de Barcelona, July 1959.

FLORENSA, Adolfo: *El barrio de Ribera y su ordenación.* Barcelona, Ayuntamiento de Barcelona, August 1959.

Picasso

BRASSAÏ: *Conversaciones.* Madrid, Aguilar, 1964.

CABANNE, Pierre: *El siglo de Picasso.* Madrid, Ministerio de Cultura, 1982.

CIRICI, Alexandre: *Picasso antes de Picasso.* Barcelona, Iberia, Joaquim Gil, 1946.

CIRLOT, Juan Eduardo: *Picasso: el nacimiento de un genio.* Barcelona, Gustavo Gili, 1972.

DAIX, Pierre: *La vie de peintre de Pablo Picasso.* Paris, Éditions su Seuil, 1977.

MALRAUX, André: *La cabeza de obsidiana.* Buenos Aires, Sur 1974.

OCAÑA, M. Teresa: *Picasso, la formació d'un geni,* 1890-1906, Barcelona, Lunwerg Editores, 1997.

PALAU i FABRE, Josep: *Picasso a Catalunya.* Barcelona, Polígrafa, 1967.

PALAU i FABRE, Josep: *Picasso vivent: 1881-1907.* Barcelona, Polígrafa, 1980.

RICHARDSON, John: *Picasso: una biografía.* vol. I. 1881-1906; vol. II 1907-1917. Madrid, Alianza, 1995 (vol. I) and 1997 (vol. II).

PENROSE, Roland: *Picasso (su vida y su obra).* Madrid, Cid, 1959.

SABARTÉS, Jaime: *Picasso. Retratos y recuerdos.* Madrid, Afrodisio Aguado, 1953.

VALLENTIN, Antonina: *Vida de Picasso.* Buenos Aires, librería Hachette, 1957.

ZERVOS, Christian: *Pablo Picasso.* Cahierd'Art, vol. I, 1932 to vol. XXXIII, 1980.

Catalogues

Catàleg de pintura i dibuix del Museu Picasso. Barcelona, Servei de Publicacions de l'Ajuntament de Barcelona, 1984.

Picasso. *Paisatges 1890-1912.* Barcelona, Museu Picasso-Lunwerg Editores, SA, 1994.

Picasso i els 4 Gats. Barcelona, Museu Picasso-Lunwerg Editores, SA, 1995.

Index to Names

■

Illustrations

■